Praise for The Waiting Place

"This is a collection of essays written by a woman with great heart, intelligence, and honesty. You might want to keep them at your bedside, like a box of literary bonbons, and read one a night as I did. Many will make you laugh out loud, at least one will make you weep, and all of them will enlarge your life in the way that reading thoughtful writing does. Bonus: no weight gain."

—Elizabeth Berg
Author, *Once Upon A Time, There Was You*

"Eileen Button's *The Waiting Place* is the shaft of sunlight on the cloudy day, a glimpse of possibility amidst difficulty. She is the wise woman of the village to whom we all repair when perspective and patience are needed."

—Philip Gulley
Author, *If the Church Were Christian*

"If Eileen Button is right—and I think she is—we find God not in some neatly resolved resolution but in our nebulous, uncertain questions. A beautiful collection of poignant and sometimes funny essays that string together like beads into an astonishingly lovely and honest memoir, *The Waiting Place* reminds us that God is everywhere—especially in the valleys of life. If you've ever prayed by a child's bedside, questioned your (or your husband's) ministry, gutted out loving your imperfect family of origin, you need the humor and insight of this book."

—Keri Wyatt Kent
Speaker and author, *Rest*

"When you finish a book and find that you miss the author the way you'd miss a friend, that's good writing. *The Waiting Place* gets better with every page and ended sooner than I wanted it to."

—Shauna Niequist
Author, *Cold Tangerines* and *Bittersweet*

"Eileen Button is a master at her craft, and *The Waiting Place* is a masterpiece. Agonizingly beautiful, side-splittingly funny, this book is the perfect companion while we wander around our own waiting places."

—CARYN DAHLSTRAND RIVADENEIRA
Author, *Grumble Hallelujah* and *Mama's Got a Fake I.D.*

"Eileen's writing style is an engaging blend of humor and poignancy. *The Waiting Place* effectively reminded me not just to slow down but to giggle while taking my foot off the proverbial gas pedal of life!"

—LISA HARPER
Women of Faith® speaker and author, *Stumbling into Grace*

"Eileen's wit and charm made her feel like an old friend by chapter 3. Whether waiting for Starbucks or chemotherapy, Eileen will add beauty and candor to all of our places of waiting."

—JENNIE ALLEN
Author, *Stuck*

"Nobody likes to wait, and most of us get restless in what seem to be stalled periods in our lives. But Eileen Button turns waiting places inside out and shows us how to approach the growth and healing that are present in such times. She teaches us to 'wait well' in this very witty, wise, and fearless memoir."

—JENNIFER GRANT
Journalist and author, *Love You More*

"Eileen Button is about to become your new best friend. Sharp, witty, and gut-wrenchingly honest, she dishes about work, love, children, husbands, and the struggle to move forward when you're forced to wait."

—KELLY FLYNN
Author, *Kids, Classrooms, and Capitol Hill*

THE
WAITING
PLACE

*Learning
to Appreciate Life's
Little Delays*

EILEEN BUTTON

THOMAS NELSON
Since 1798

NASHVILLE   DALLAS   MEXICO CITY   RIO DE JANEIRO

Published in Nashville, Tennessee, by Thomas Nelson. Thomas Nelson is a registered trademark of Thomas Nelson, Inc.

Thomas Nelson, Inc. titles may be purchased in bulk for educational, business, fund-raising, or sales promotional use. For information, please e-mail SpecialMarkets@ThomasNelson.com.

Scripture quotations are taken from the New King James Version®. © 1982 by Thomas Nelson, Inc. Used by permission. All rights reserved.

Oh, the Places You'll Go! by Dr. Seuss,™ and © by Dr. Seuss Enterprises L.P. 1990. Used by permission of Random House Children's Books, a division of Random House, Inc.

"This is Your Life" by Jonathan Foreman. © 2003 Meadowgreen Music Company (ASCAP) Sugar Pete Songs (ASCAP) (adm. at EMICMGPublishing.com). All rights reserved. Used by permission.

Names, characterizations, and details in some of the author's anecdotes and stories have been changed to protect identities.

Some of the essays in this volume originally appeared in the *Flint Journal* and *Christianity Today: Gifted for Leadership* and have been edited for inclusion here.

Library of Congress Cataloging-in-Publication Data

Button, Eileen, 1966–
    The waiting place: learning to appreciate life's little delays / Eileen Button.
       p. cm.
    ISBN 978-0-8499-4625-7 (pbk.)
    1. Expectation (Psychology)—Religious aspects—Christianity. 2. Waiting (Philosophy)
3. Patience—Religious aspects—Christianity. 4. Providence and government of God—Christianity. 5. Trust in God—Christianity. I. Title. II. Title: Learning to appreciate life's little delays.
    BV4647.E93B88 2011
    248.4—dc22   2011003724

Printed in the United States of America

11 12 13 14 15 RRD 9 8 7 6 5 4 3 2 1

To my husband, Brad,
who has waited alongside me
for more than half my life
and never once let go of my hand.

—◊—

You can get so confused
that you'll start in to race
down long wiggled roads at a break-necking pace
and grind on for miles across weirdish wild space,
headed, I fear, toward a most useless place.

The Waiting Place . . .

—Dr. Seuss, *Oh, the Places You'll Go!*

.

Contents

Contents

Acknowledgments

—⟋⟍—

They say the writing life is a lonely one, best suited for the quiet and introverted. Had I believed that, I never would have attempted it. Fortunately, I've been surrounded by the coolest kind of people who have encouraged me and dared me to tell the truth. I'm especially grateful for:

Debbie Wickwire, my kind-hearted, inspiring editor at Thomas Nelson, along with Sue Ann Jones, a masterful weaver of words.

David Sanford and Karen Neumair, my terrific agents at Credo Communications, who have made the adventure so much stinkin' fun.

Kelly Flynn, brilliant writer, faithful accountability partner, and trusted friend. I cannot imagine traveling this long, wiggled road without her.

Caryn Dahlstrand Rivadeneira, who believed in this book before I thought I had anything to say.

Marsha Bolton Rivers, Susan Carroll, Lori Casadonte, Rilla

Crothers, Sarah Easton, Mary Flaherty, Monica Martin, Theresa Shadrix, Vanessa Stallkamp, and Jennie Welliver. They read my stuff, asked the tough questions, and shared both laughter and tears.

Mary Higginbottom, Shirley Heritage, Johnnie Jones, and Cindy Lo'Ree, who treat me like a treasured coworker at the Davison Branch of the Genesee District Library.

Marjory Raymer, Barb Modrack, Tony Dearing, and Vera Hogan, present and past editors at the *Flint Journal*, along with faithful readers of the weekly column.

Brad Button and our extraordinary children, Stephen, Kristina, and Jordan; along with my dad, Clark Gable; my mom, Bonnie Gable; and my in-laws, Winston and Georgia Button. We are a motley crew, but our love for one another is exquisite.

Finally, I am grateful to God, who so obviously has a fabulous sense of humor. I'm thankful he joins me in the waiting place, even when it grows dark and I get scared and lose my way.

1

THE WAITING PLACE

I am waiting for the day to end. Just end.

I am sitting on the left side of my red couch, flipping through the most recent edition of *Newsweek*. Since I am a newspaper columnist, I am hoping—praying, actually—that an idea for my next column will jump out of the magazine's pages and smack me in the head.

Come on. There must be something *in here worth writing about,* I think as I scan the boring stories.

Most of the time I have a lot to say. In fact, I have an opinion on just about everything, which is a very good trait to have if you're a columnist. But today, I'm in a slump. And I know from

Dr. Seuss's *Oh, the Places You'll Go!* that "when you're in a Slump, / you're not in for much fun. / Un-slumping yourself / is not easily done."

The fact is, I'm stuck in "a most useless place. The Waiting Place." It's a wobbly place to be.

It's March. I live in mid-Michigan, where I am surrounded by thousands of disillusioned auto workers, many of whom have lost their jobs in recent years. The weather is a horrible mixture of ice, rain, and snow. Although I am a runner (who runs mostly in her mind), I haven't run in several months. My diet consists mostly of cookies. My pants are tight (go figure), and my gluteus maximus is maximizing itself. It has an obvious agenda to take over the entire back side of my body. After it accomplishes that there is no doubt in my mind it is going for world domination.

If someone asked me, "If you could be anywhere in the world right now, where would you be?" I would answer, "In bed." The fact that I would choose flannel sheets over, say, Italy is more than a little concerning to this Tigger-like, energetic woman.

My eleven-year-old daughter, Kristina, is home from school, sick. She's curled up on the couch next to me, engrossed in her latest book. A bowl of green grapes sits between us, and we take turns reaching into it and popping fruit into our mouths. I might not know where my next column will come from, but it's nice to be here with my little girl.

Kristina is sick but not too sick. Together we're bored but not too bored. I reason that our boredom is even a little healthy. That it's a good thing to just sit and read and think and wonder every once in a while.

Kristina breaks the silence as she peeks up over her book at me. "Can I ask you a question, Mom?"

"Sure," I answer. She's reading *My Little Red Book*, which is a wonderful collection of personal essays all written about first-menstruation experiences. I know that a book comprised solely of first-period stories sounds odd, but it is truly terrific, funny, and poignant. Kristina has my full attention as I put down the *Newsweek* and look into her beautiful face. I am ready to spend the entire day talking about what it means to become a woman while her brothers, Stephen and Jordan, are at school. In my daughter's eyes, I soon will be Mother of the Year.

"Well," she says. "Uh . . . is this what you do all day?"

I'm taken aback by her question and laugh nervously. "What? You mean, like, sit here? Oh, no, no. Gosh, no," I say.

"Good. Because if this is what you do all day, it would drive me crazy!" she says. "So, what *do* you do all day?"

Suddenly I glimpse myself through her eyes and see a middle-aged woman who appears to be a little lost while her husband works and her kids go to school. My stomach turns, and I have to push down the defenses that rise up within me. I am tempted to harangue long and hard about the fact that I am a newspaper columnist and an adjunct professor and a mom of three *who makes dinner every single stinkin' night!* Plus, I'm a pastor's wife who loves her husband but often dislikes his job that overshadows our life together.

I am also a neighbor, a sister, a daughter, and a friend. I volunteer at the local library, church, and school. I do the laundry, clean the toilets, sweep the floors, weed the garden, and wash the dog. I drive kids around in my proverbial minivan (a vehicle so unremarkable we call her the Stealth Bomber) to school, lessons, practices, and doctors' appointments. In short, *I'm freaking amazing!*

But I don't say any of that. Instead, I calmly say, "Oh, I work. You know, I write. I grade papers. I plan lessons for class. I don't just hang around here and sit on the couch."

"Well, you can work now if you want to," she says.

"I know. But I just . . . I want to be here with you."

"Okay," she says as she turns back to her book. "It's just that, I'm fine. So you don't have to stop whatever it is you normally do."

"Uh-huh," I say, and I look blankly at the pages before me. *So this is what my life has come to.* I am utterly defeated.

—⁓⁓⁓—

When my three children were old enough to watch *Spy Kids* but young enough to still be gullible, they became convinced that my husband, Brad, and I were spies for the US government. They believed we did our spy work while they slept cozily in their beds. When they asked us if we were members of the CIA, we sometimes said yes, and they accused us of lying. But when we said no, they thought we were lying, too. Either way, they were convinced that whatever it was that we did while they were sleeping was much more exotic than simply snoozing. We were their heroes.

My children are no longer gullible. More often than not they call our bluff. It is hard to admit that the person I am at this very moment—the woman who sits soberly on the left side of her couch holding *Newsweek* in one hand and a bitter cup of lukewarm coffee in the other—is not the person I meant to become. Certainly I'm not acting like the mom I want my daughter to believe she has. I want her to think that I am adventurous, creative, inspired, and important. Instead, I feel cautious, vulnerable, a little lazy, and just plain stuck.

I never dreamed of becoming the mother who kisses her children good-bye as she sends them off to school in the morning, presses the Pause button on her life, and resumes living once her offspring return home. After all, I am the mother who unashamedly allowed—even encouraged—her children to believe she was the cunning, cool-headed CIA agent who flew to Moscow and back as they slept or went to school. Certainly I never just stay home.

Kristina looks at me nonjudgmentally, but her eyes plead for me to do something with my sorry life. Isn't there *something* on this random Tuesday in March that I need to do? Isn't there *someplace* (Cuba, perhaps) that I need to go?

Instead, I am trapped in the waiting place. And so it is here, on the left side of my very comfortable couch, that this book is born.

—◊◊◊—

The Waiting Place is for people like me who get stuck in their precious, mundane, gorgeous, absurd lives. It is for those who work hard at the "business of living" only to find that they seem to be caught in one long, boring meeting. (The kind held around a long, laminated dark table in a windowless room where the boss, who forgot to bring donuts, is giving a PowerPoint presentation that includes about fifteen thousand pie charts.)

It's for those who wake up one day and find themselves repeatedly sighing and thinking, *This is* so *not the life I dreamed of living.* It's also for those who wonder what is worse: to remain in the day-in, day-out lives they have created or to risk it all and make a change, even if that change results in falling on their faces.

The waiting place is never cozy. In fact, when we find ourselves there, most of us try like heck to escape. While stuck in traffic, we take the nearest off-ramp and find an alternate route. While waiting at the deli, we gather a few more groceries from adjacent aisles so as not to waste time. While waiting at the mind-sucking Department of Motor Vehicles, we take a number and watch the numbers click, click, click until we are called to the desk. (Effects of the torturous wait at the DMV can be seen in virtually everyone's pitiful driver's license picture.)

Sometimes our inability to wait has more tragic implications:

+ While waiting to grow up, we forget to embrace our childhoods.
+ While waiting to lose weight, we fail to enjoy the youthfulness of our bodies.
+ While waiting for true love, we forget to relish our freedom. (Or worse, we settle for second best.)
+ While waiting to have children, we forget to nurture and enjoy the love and freedom of a childless marriage.
+ While waiting for our children to grow, we forget to notice their beauty as infants, toddlers, children, and teens. We fail to burn the memory of them into our souls.
+ While waiting for a loved one to get well (or to die), we fail

to appreciate the days—even those filled with sickness and medications—we have with one another.

The following essays breathe life into common (and not so common) waiting places. I hope you find yourself in these pages and conclude, as I have, that some of the most priceless gifts can be discovered while waiting for something else.

I am absolutely convinced that some of the most beautiful things happen if we are willing to quiet our hearts, lean into the waiting place, and listen to what it tells us. When we do, we will often be astonished by what it has to say.

2

WHISPERING WALLS

I am waiting for a place called home.

I've driven by this house a thousand times over the last thirty years. When my kids are in the car with me, I slow down, point, and say, "There it is, kids. That's the house I grew up in."

They glance and say, "Oh, yeah . . . ," and quickly go back to their own thoughts.

I'm never too disappointed by their response. After all, my childhood house in East Rochester, New York, (population sixty-six hundred) is not much to look at. The corner lot is tiny and comprised mostly of dirt. The once-white siding on the small two-story house is brownish gray from decades of harsh western New York winters. In this part of town, no one ever power-washes his home or contracts with ChemLawn to spray her grass. Here, residents are much more concerned about basic survival—a roof overhead, food on the table, a working car in the driveway, and a source of steady income.

I am the only one in my family who has moved out of state. My mom, dad, and two sisters all live within a few miles of each other. This fact often makes me terribly jealous and more than a little sad. I travel back to the east side of Rochester for most of the important stuff: weddings, major holidays, funerals.

But it's the ordinary, everyday stuff I miss the most: Sunday dinners . . . the Buffalo Bills versus Miami Dolphins football game . . . taking my sisters to lunch for their birthdays . . . hanging out just because we can . . . running out of things to say . . . stopping by a sister's home without her thinking she should pick up her house and clean her toilets first. My heart longs for these simple things.

The unspoken rule for just about every family I know is this: the one who moves away must also be the one who visits. I don't mind being the one who hauls my family to Rochester because I want my kids to know this place. I'm happy to trek back several times a year to be in the presence of the people who have known me the longest and love me the most. Sure, I wish they'd come to visit me more often and take the time to understand my life as I do theirs. In spite of that, whenever anyone asks me about my home, this is the place I think of first.

It's hard to believe that this is the same small town my high school classmates and I could hardly wait to leave. How ironic it is to no longer feel that way. Instead, I feel like I've been missing something beautiful all along: the knowledge of which deli in town sells the best homemade kielbasa or pepperoni bread . . . the awkwardness of banging into an old boyfriend at the grocery store . . . the weirdness of watching former classmates' kids walk across the stage at graduation. Every town is unique, and heartstrings are pulled tightly around it, even if it's hard to explain exactly why.

My childhood house is located halfway between my dad's trailer and my sister's home. As I drive past it en route to Susie's, my heart leaps when I see the For Sale sign from Canal Walk Realtors sitting crookedly in the yard. I memorize the phone number and the Realtor's name.

"Hey, Susie," I say, walking through her front door, down the hallway, and into her aroma-filled kitchen. "Do you want to go see a house with me?"

"What house?" she asks, stirring the pasta for tonight's dinner.

"*Our* house. The Apple Street house. You wanna see it? It's for sale."

"You want to buy the Apple Street house?" she asks, incredulous.

"No, of course I don't want to buy it. I just want to see it. Will you go with me?"

Over the years, Susie and I have dreamed together about the possibility of seeing the house again. "Are you serious?" she says.

"Yeah. But only if the Realtor will show it to us."

"I'll go. Absolutely."

I grab her phone and head into the quiet of her upstairs, rehearsing what I will say to the Realtor when he answers the phone. *If* he answers the phone.

"Frank DeCiantis," a man's voice says.

"Uh, yes. Hi. My name is Eileen, and . . . well, I'm interested in seeing one of the houses you have listed, the one on Apple Street. But I don't want to buy it."

"*O-kaay*," he says hesitantly.

"I know it sounds crazy, but . . . I grew up there, and my sister and I have always wondered what it would be like to see it again. Since it's on the market . . . ," I say as my confidence tanks. "Gosh, I'm so sorry to ask you this. I don't want to waste your time. I'm sure you're busy and . . ."

"Well, the house has sold, but it's no problem. I'd be happy to show it to you. When do you want to see it?"

I swallow and hold my breath. "Now?"

I hear him shuffling papers. Then he says, "Meet me there in twenty minutes."

—⁂—

It's hard to believe it's been thirty years since Susie and I stood on the cement stoop of our eight-hundred-square-foot childhood home. She and I have both bought and renovated a few houses as adults, but no one has given similar attention to this place. We grip the black wrought-iron railing with its chipped paint, and I can almost hear my mother banging her clapperless brass bell against it, calling us to dinner. Frank unlocks the familiar side door, and Susie shoots me a look in anticipation. Although we've talked about doing this, we never thought we'd get the chance to walk through these doors again.

I can hardly wait to see the inside, but I'm a little nervous about what we will find. What if memories slam back at me and knock me off my feet? But I'm equally nervous about standing here on the steps, exposed for all the neighbors to see. There is very little space between houses, so every car pulling into a driveway, every person standing at the door, is noticed. I can't help the feeling that Fran Kokinda is watching me from her kitchen window across the street, even though she died seven months ago. She watched our family from the shadows of that window for thirteen years. It's hard to imagine she's gone.

Susie and I follow Frank into the kitchen and into the wrinkle in time. The worn-out egg-salad-patterned kitchen floor has been covered with different linoleum, but the pine cupboards, worn red countertop, 1970s refrigerator, and mustard-colored telephone (complete with an extra-long, stretched-out cord) are, remarkably, unchanged.

I'm shocked to find the same brown, nubby carpeting covering the living room floor. That carpet was wicked-ugly in the seventies, and it hasn't improved in the last three decades. I look around the tiny ten-by-twelve room and shake my head at the memory of one of my mother's enormous Christmas trees stuffed into the northwest corner. We had good Christmases here. Mom was the Christmas queen who loved shopping for and wrapping her Santa-sized load. Dad didn't share her enthusiasm for the holidays but was content to watch his girls tear open presents on Christmas morning.

Frank opens the door to the enclosed front porch, and I become dizzy with nostalgia. The damp-wood smell is exactly the same after all these years. This is the place where I wrote my very first story, where I read and loved Judy Blume's *Are You There God? It's Me, Margaret*, and where I spent hours perfecting my ability to raise one eyebrow.

Flooded with reluctant hope, I approach one of the windows, pull back the worn lace curtain, and find the thing I'm looking for. Etched into the windowsill in a child's handwriting is my other sister's name: MARY.

"Look at this, Sue," I say, stepping away from the curtain to show her our sister's name.

"Oh my gosh. Are you kidding me? You know, she got in a lot of trouble for doing that, even though I was the one who carved it."

"I know. Weird, huh?"

Suddenly I want to break free from Frank, this wonderful man who is spending his valuable time with Susie and me instead of with his own family. He is talking about our town, school, and mutual acquaintances. I answer back, but it's difficult to talk and listen because I don't know how to manage our conversation and walk down memory lane at the same time.

I'm tempted to grab my sister's hand and run upstairs to our bedroom where we used to play dress-up. We'll squat down in one of its corners playing hide-and-seek and whisper, "*Sh!* Be quiet. He'll never find us here."

I want pink-and-white-striped wallpaper to still cover our walls, and our beds to be waiting for us to crawl beneath the covers with our flashlights so we can make scary faces with light and shadows. We'll make believe we're movie stars and once again pretend that our boyfriends are Leif Garrett and Andy Gibb. We'll jump between the beds to avoid the imaginary alligators swimming beneath us—until Dad yells at us from the stairway, "Girls! Stop that jumpin' on the beds!" Then we'll jump a little quieter.

Instead of acting like a lunatic, I pretend to be an adult. Susie and I follow Frank upstairs so he can show us the second floor we used to know so well. We peek into our impossibly tiny bathroom, which is so narrow it cannot fit a full-size tub, and wonder aloud how on earth the five of us managed to get ready in the morning. We enter the bedroom my sisters and I shared and marvel that the room was built without the "luxury" of a closet. We stand inside the empty space that was my parents' bedroom and remember that our parents, who have now been divorced for more years than they were married, once loved each other here.

We head downstairs, walk through the living room and kitchen, and step down rickety steps into the basement. The distinct smell of mold permeates the air. I see the cover of the drain pipe that once came off, making it possible for the rats from the salvage yard across the street to enter our basement and eat a few of the pet guinea pigs we kept down here. Most people hate rats; my hatred is personal.

"I don't believe it," I say, shaking off my rat memory and making my way to the laundry area. "This is the same washing machine."

"Impossible," Frank says.

"I'm sure of it," I say, reaching toward the unit. I remember exactly how to turn it on. The water begins spraying into the empty tub. "See?"

"Huh. That's pretty amazing."

"Yeah. Makes you appreciate the way they used to make appliances, doesn't it?"

"Sure does," he says.

And on that note, I know my wrinkle in time has ended. It's time to go.

We stand outside again in the crisp March air. Frank and I figure out ways our childhoods intersected. It turns out that during many of the years my family lived in this house, Frank was our paperboy.

"It's kinda funny that you lived here. You know, my parents always wondered if I would come back alive when I delivered newspapers to this street," he says.

"Yeah. It was pretty rough," I say, thinking back to the times I played cops and robbers with neighborhood kids who spent time at juvenile detention centers.

"Oh, yeah," he says, laughing. "I think it had the highest concentration of German shepherds in the entire county."

"What a kid will do for a few extra bucks, right?"

"No kidding."

Before my sister and I leave, I take one last look at the yard and the street. Funny how it seemed so much bigger when I was a child. Today I feel as humongous as Alice after she falls down the rabbit hole into a miniature wonderland.

It occurs to me that you never really forget your childhood home. The walls, décor, furniture, neighborhood—they all shape us, like it or not. The memories, good and bad, whisper to us through time, "This is who you are." Our childhoods set up residence in our souls. We might try to leave them behind, but they insist on having their say.

As Frederick Buechner movingly wrote in *Telling the Truth*, "You can kiss your family and friends good-bye and put miles between you, but at the same time you carry them with you in your heart, your mind, your stomach, because you do not just live in a world but a world lives in you."

Over the years, I've listened to my childhood as it whispered poignant, painful, and humorous reminders into my heart, giving me the strength to withstand all that would be ahead of me. It also helped me search the waiting place until I discovered beauty, joy, and hilarity. Some might say it has produced a certain eccentricity, giving me the fluorescent rose-colored glasses through which I experience the world. So be it. I'm not interested in living my crazy, absurd, gorgeous life any other way.

—∿∿—

Susie and I linger outside with Frank, finding it strangely difficult to leave. "This tree is spectacular in the springtime," I tell him, pointing to the still barren tree in the corner of the tiny lot.

"Cherry, right?"

"Uh-huh . . . but it's special. Different," I say, but I can't remember why. Perhaps it's special because I used to swing from its branches. Like my childhood, the tree was once mine.

3

CURLING IRON CHRONICLES

I am waiting for Mom to finish styling my hair.

In the holiday-Catholic family of my childhood, Jesus is not only the Son of God. He also is a swear word. When my parents are really, really angry, they say his name as three distinct words. These are steady, angry syllables usually hollered with the accompaniment of a heavy fist pounding the kitchen table three times.

A number of things can prompt this outburst from my parents. Perhaps the basement floods. Or one of us girls leaves the Super Sugar Crisp box open and a small ant army overtakes the cupboard.

Or one of us tries to make a Coke-sicle in a drinking glass, and the soda spills all over the inside of the freezer. Whatever the spark that causes the eruption, whenever my sisters and I hear Jesus' name shouted, we know it's time to disappear.

———

I am sitting in front of my mother on her double bed as she curls and styles my hair. At eleven years old, I am certainly old enough to be doing my own hair, but Mom isn't quite ready to let go of the morning ritual she loves. Mom is a girly girl to the millionth degree, and she is thrilled to have three daughters, in part because we give her three extra heads of hair to curl, tease, spray, and twist into unfathomable poofdom. Well into adulthood, people who knew me as a child say, "Oh, you're one of Bonnie's daughters. She always had you girls looking so pretty. Do you remember your ringlets?"

"Oh yes, I remember the ringlets," I say as I laugh and try really hard not to roll my eyes. "Everyone remembers the ringlets."

Ringlet Road is paved with many tears. After sleeping all night in pink sponge curlers, my sisters and I have "curler races" to see who can untwist the rollers from our long hair the fastest. Lined up in front of my mother's bureau mirror, my sisters and I assume our positions as Mom says, "Ready, get set, *go!*" Then, with fingers flying, we unclip and unravel the curlers, allowing them to fall onto the doily on the dresser. My hair is the thickest, so as usual I end up losing. I've always been a little too competitive; I hate losing anything, even silly things like curler races.

———

"Done!" one of my sisters yell, positively beaming over her curler race victory.

"No fair!" I yell back with five curlers still stuck in my tangled hair and my eyes welling up with tears.

"Oh, Eileen, don't be such a sore loser," Mom says.

"But I have more curlers than they do," I say. "It's not fair."

"Don't be ridiculous. Now, who's first?" One of us scrambles into position in front of her so she can pull our long, wildly curly hair into two perfect ponytails. She then twists them around her finger, stopping to spray them with Aqua Net at every rotation. Once the hairspray dries, Mom carefully pulls her finger out of the ringlets, which hang like Hostess Ho Hos along the sides of our heads.

At school, boys stick their fingers up into my ringlets and yank them down. Inevitably, by the time I return home, one ringlet is several inches longer than the others. It isn't easy being a ringletted girl, but beauty demands sacrifice.

Thankfully, a few years later, as I sit in front of Mom on her bed, my ringlet days are over. These days, she works from the crown downward through my short, layered hair, smoothing under each section with the hot, metal curling iron. Although she tries to be careful, the curling iron often singes the tops of my ears and my forehead. Hearing my skin sizzle, I cry out from the sting. I learn at a very young age that beauty means pain. My hairstyle hides the burns.

Mom combs out the warm coils of hair and blends them together. The resultant hairdo resembles a wig, which is why the horrible kids at my school call out, "Wig lady! Wig lady! Wigs for sale!" as we wait for the morning bell to summon us into the building. I pretend I can't hear them.

This infuriates them, so they say it louder, to my face. "*Wig lady!! Wig lady!! Wigs for sale!!*"

I smile into their mocking eyes and try to go along with the joke, but I want to run away. Or at least have normal eleven-year-old hair.

When I tell my mother about the name calling, she says, "Oh, Eileen, just ignore them. Your hair is beautiful. They're just jealous of you."

But I know that's not completely true. After all, I have the exact same hairstyle as Mrs. McKay, the strict-but-cool seventh-grade English teacher who drives a baby-blue Pontiac Firebird. Mrs. McKay is in her sixties. Which means I have sixty-year-old hair.

My mother, undeterred by such thoughts, is in her glory at the head of her bed, where she is propped up by pillows and surrounded by her styling paraphernalia. While she works her styling magic, she and I listen to the local pop radio station that plays our favorite songs and asks us the Question of the Day.

This morning, as I sit before my mother, the radio announcer says, "Okay, folks, today's question is this: Who was the most loved man of all time?"

Mom and I take turns guessing. "John F. Kennedy," she says.

"How about Elvis?" I say.

"Ooh, Elvis. Yeah, it might be Elvis. Or maybe one of the Beatles."

I don't know much about the Beatles, but I know they are a very big deal. I've seen the *Ed Sullivan Show* reruns with all the girls screaming when those four boys with bowl haircuts take the stage. It terrifies me to see so many girls freaking out over a bunch of boys. Besides, I think the Bee Gees are way better.

Listeners begin calling in to the station with their guesses, taking ours by proxy.

"Elvis?" a caller asks.

"Nope. Thanks for calling," the DJ says.

"John F. Kennedy?"

"Nope. Thanks for calling."

"Martin Luther King Jr.?"

"Nope. Thanks for calling."

Finally, a caller guesses correctly. The most loved man in the history of the world is Jesus Christ.

"Hm, *that's* interesting," my mother says. "Okay, Eileen, turn and face me. I need to finish your bangs."

I reposition my body to face my mother, and my eye catches the crucifix that hangs over her bed. Looking up at his broken body, I feel a little ashamed that I didn't guess Jesus Christ. After all, I love him a lot, and I know he loves me. As I bow my bangs before my mother, Jesus bows his head toward us. I wonder if he's disappointed that I didn't guess he is the most loved man of all time.

Several minutes pass as I contemplate hearing the name Jesus Christ on the same station that is now playing Rod Stewart's "Hot Legs." My mother is absorbed in her own thoughts. Most likely, she's wishing the radio station would play a song by Neil Diamond or Barry Manilow.

Finally, I say what's on my mind. "Jesus Christ," I say. "I never thought of that."

Whack! My mother's hand stings the side of my face, and I scream from the shock of it. Stunned by her own response at her oldest daughter's "swearing," she narrows her eyes and demands, "What did you say?"

My eyes well with tears as I hold my face in my hands. "I . . . I said, 'I never thought of that.'"

My mother looks at me squarely. "That's not all you said, young lady."

"Yes, I did!" I insist, and I start to cry. "I said, 'Jesus Christ.' You know . . . the radio. The DJ said he was the most loved man of all time."

Mom bursts into nervous laughter and starts apologizing. "I'm so sorry, Eileen. I thought you were saying, 'Jesus Christ' in a swearing kinda way. Oh, please stop crying. I didn't mean to," she pleads as she reaches for me, hoping to hug away my pain. I am, after all, a "good girl." I'm not the kind of child who gets slapped across the face.

"I'm okay," I choke out, now sobbing. "I . . . was . . . just . . . surprised." Reluctantly, I lean into her.

Six years later, I place my life fully into God's hands.

—⚊⚊—

My adult self often thinks about the little girl with sixty-year-old hair who was slapped for saying, "Jesus Christ." I want to tell her to look up and fix her eyes on Jesus. I want her to know that he will soon mean so much more to her than just a swear word. One day, he will become an unexpected friend and a surprising confidante.

He will listen as she pours out her grief, anger, and frustration without delivering a single stinging slap in response. And he will think she's beautiful—not because of her hairstyle, but because he knows her heart.

4

LIFTING FOG

I am waiting for the fish to bite.

I am fishing with my dad, sitting in a white rowboat in the middle of a small lake in the Adirondack Mountains. It's eight o'clock in the morning, and I've already been in the boat for three hours. If the fish start showing our lures some interest, we'll be out here a few hours longer. The sun is shining, but the August wind is surprisingly chilly. Plus, I have to go to the bathroom. (Oh my word, I *really* have to go to the bathroom.) Still, although I'm only twelve years old, there's no place else I'd rather be.

I suppress a yawn and allow it to fill up the back of my throat. My eyes water at the attempt. I don't want my dad to see that I am tired because I don't want him to take me back to the cabin, where the rest of our family waits for us. This is my time with Dad, and I'm protective of it.

Later, Mom will want to take my grandmother, my sisters, and me on an adventure into Lake Placid. We will do touristy things, buy Harlequin romances from the dime store, and eat tuna fish sandwiches at a local diner. If we're lucky, we'll go to the top of White Face Mountain. My mom loves an adventure and so do I. But my dad loves to fish. Since fishing is one of the very few things my dad and I get to do alone together, I want the moments to last.

As the story goes, I was two years old when my dad informed my mom that he was taking me out for an ice cream cone. Happily, my mother went to collect her purse. "No, Bonnie," my dad said. "Alone."

"Alone? Why?"

"I just want to take her by myself."

Mom got upset and started crying. She ended up coming along. I've been told that story dozens of times throughout my life, and I always come to the same conclusion. I wish my dad would have stood his ground and taken me out for ice cream by himself. I wish he would have been given the chance to figure out what to do with my tears when I licked the vanilla ice cream too happily, causing it to tumble out of my cone and splat on the sidewalk. I wish he would have been the one to clean my sticky face with a napkin. Perhaps then we would have done other things together: playgrounds, walks, dinner, movies. Instead, I wait for my once-a-year fishing trip. It never feels like enough, but it's what I have.

In the boat, Dad and I don't talk because we don't want to scare off the fish with voices that can be heard under water. Instead, we toss one another knowing glances when we suspect we're casting into a promising spot or if we believe the seaweed is too thick for our lures. Although I'll fish with whatever lure Dad ties onto my line, I prefer to use a Red Devil. It is heavier and causes my pole to bend slightly, making me feel like I've caught a fish even when I'm only reeling in my line. Unfortunately, it also tends to be more unpredictable than other lures. Its weight causes it to have a mind of its own.

Small waves lap against the boat as we drift thirty feet from shore. My palms sweat a little as I get my pole ready to cast. I hold my breath and exhale a "Thank you, God" as the Red Devil plops perfectly just beneath a small tree that juts out from the shore, hovering like an umbrella over the water. I look over at my dad, who is reeling in his line. He purses his lips together, squints his eyes, and nods his head proudly. When I look into his eyes, I see my own. Bright blue. Intense. Smiling.

It's that very look I've been waiting for. His pride-filled face says everything I need to hear. It's what motivates me to peel my body from my bed at five o'clock in the morning and what will compel me to repeatedly cast my fishing line until the early afternoon. Every year I enter this waiting place under the pretense of wanting to catch fish. But what I really want is my dad—all of him—to myself. My dad's approval is more thrilling to me than catching a twenty-four-inch pike or a nineteen-inch bass. Later, we'll return to the camp with stories about the one that got away, but I will have his nonverbal praise tucked into my heart.

A family vacation with grandparents (my mother's father and stepmother) at their Adirondack cabin conjures up quaint images like those to be found in the glossy pages of *Country Living* magazine, but ours is a blue-collar kind of vacation. At the camp, there is no indoor plumbing, electricity, or running water. Instead, there is an outhouse located in the woods a good twenty feet from the cabin; everyone gets constipated on our annual vacations because no one can tolerate the outhouse for long. The smell is suffocating, and the militant black flies think they own the place.

My sisters and I are especially terrified by the outhouse because it's wicked-dark. It's also impossible to peer into the hole to see what animal might be lurking there. I'm not sure what kind of creature enjoys sloshing around in the muck, but I have a full-blown phobia of snakes and am absolutely convinced that one is coiled on top of all the excrement, waiting for me to sit down so it can spring up and bite my rear. I whimper and pray, *Oh, God, please don't let it bite me . . . please don't let it bite me*, the entire time I'm seated.

The miniature hunting cabin measures fifteen by twenty-five feet and is tucked deep into the woods. Inside, the main room contains a wall of kitchen counters, a table that seats ten (with everyone's elbows touching), a propane-powered refrigerator, an old convertible couch, a woodstove, and a Victrola. Behind two flowery-curtained doorways, two teeny bedrooms overflow with their single full beds and ancient dressers. My grandparents sleep in one room. My parents sleep in the other. *Cozy* is one word to describe it. *Cramped* is another.

My two sisters and I sleep in the living room on a mouse-infested convertible couch. We never complain, although we fight over the middle. It's the warmest spot and we figure that, if a mouse is going to run across us, the middle sleeper will be the most protected.

Our fears are not unfounded. A few years ago, a mouse got into bed with my parents and ran up the length of my father's leg. My father hollered for Jesus as he leaped from the covers, the Lord's name shouted in the familiar harsh, accented syllables awakening the household. Stumbling, his body slammed into the dresser, and my mother's many toiletries—hairspray, deodorant, nail-polish remover, liquid makeup, and rouge—tumbled onto the floor and rolled around the room.

My father's racket woke the entire cabin. From the next room over, my grandfather jokingly echoed Dad's shout-out to Jesus.

Then my grandparents' laughter bounced off the walls, making my sisters and me giggle right along with them. My mother, who loves to laugh, could not get control of herself even after my father had liberated himself from the rodent. Mom's laughter would subside, and we'd try to fall back asleep, but she'd burst into fits of laughter once again, and the entire cabin would laugh along with her.

"That's enough, Bonnie," my dad would say. "It's over now."

But Dad's pleas just made her laugh harder. Eventually he gave up, and we all got tired. Still, every few minutes my mom could be heard laughing alone.

That audacious mouse managed to produce the most laughter my family ever shared together.

—⟶⟵—

On fishing day, Dad whispers my name to wake me, and I slip out from under the covers. It's always still dark and almost impossible to see anything. Although it's summer, I'm wearing two pairs of socks because the temperature inside the cabin often dips into the forties. The floor is like ice beneath my feet, and I hurry over to my suitcase to pull on layers of warm clothing. I hope the sun will warm the lake enough that I'll be able to peel the layers off as we fish.

I follow my dad down to the boat. Together we pile the tackle box, fishing poles, candy bars, beers for him, and Pepsis for me into the boat and push off into the water. The only sound is the scraping of the aluminum boat against the muddy bottom as we leave. It is still quite dark, and the air smells heavily of pine. Fog hangs thick over the water. As we move through it, the shore eerily disappears.

"Where are we going, Dad?" I whisper, and he points down the lake and starts the outboard motor—the same one he spent weeks taking apart, oiling, and repairing in our driveway at home. He's relieved when it roars to life. This moment is my father's idea of perfection.

The sun rises quickly, and the fog begins to lift like a theater curtain off the water's surface, revealing what our family calls "God's country." Dad slows and then cuts the motor, and we drift into a cove that feels like it's teeming with starving fish that will only be satisfied by our lures. We quietly row closer to the shore, within casting distance. Then we cast toward a protruding rock where we are certain the big one waits. We hear a fish break the surface of the murky water, and we cast toward the ripples his jump leaves behind. Over and over again, we cast . . . reel in . . . cast . . . reel in. The rhythm erases any sense of time yet inexplicably connects us.

Every once in a while, hungry for Dad's praise, I make an especially risky cast. This time I spot a tree that juts out at a forty-five-degree angle, casting an expansive shadow over the water's surface. I'm convinced there is an adult continuing-education class for pike being held directly beneath the branches. I reposition myself, grab the line, click the reel into place, and expertly cast toward it.

Midcast, my heavy Red Devil grows wings, flies into the tree, drapes over a branch, and sways five feet above the water. I don't want to ruin the fishing spot by having to collect the lure, so, with a swift jerk and a prayer, I yank the lure upward, hoping it will fly back through the tree and plunk into the water.

My efforts do greater damage. The hook snags and the lure quickly becomes a red and white ornament dangling from a branch about ten feet above the water. As it twists in the breeze, the silver side catches the sun and the reflection sparkles across the lake. If it weren't my lure, it might be pretty.

I shoot my dad a pathetic look, but he's too preoccupied staring at the nested Red Devil to look at me. He swears as he reels in his lure, lays the pole in the boat, and grabs for the oars.

"Sorry, Dad."

As we near the shore, I imagine the adult education class of fish being hastily dismissed. "Eileen, reel in the line!"

"Okay." I have to spin the reel fast because the line's slack is landing on the water. The tree is quickly upon us, and we both have to duck under its leaves. A sharp branch slides down my back, penetrating my sweatshirt and scratching me. I free myself as I tug on the line, all the while praying to God that he will free the stupid Red Devil. Although I'm sure he has bigger things to worry about than my lure, I pray some more. God knows exactly how much Dad and his approval mean to me.

———

"I wish you hadn't done that," Dad says.

"I know. I thought I could yank it down."

"Well, it's too late now. That thing is up there," he says, peering through the branches.

I'm willing to do just about anything to get it down. Anything. "I could climb the tree."

"Don't be ridiculous. You're *not* going to climb that tree."

He retrieves his nail clippers from his tackle box, cuts my line, and begins rowing away from the tree. I brush leaves and a few sticks out of my hair as I watch my lureless fishing line dance in the breeze. The emancipated Red Devil mocks me as we leave it behind. *You failed.* Although Dad's disappointment presses heavily upon me, I resolve to try again. Next time I'll play it safer; I'm determined to be redeemed in my father's eyes.

Dad starts the motor, and we move toward another promising cove. I still have to go to the bathroom, but I decide I've inconvenienced him enough for one day. I tell myself to keep still, cast carefully, and wait. Sitting in the bow, I turn my face into the wind and blink back the tears I don't want him to see. Like I said, Dad never figured out what to do with my tears. He lives in a household filled with women. The least I can do is toughen up and be like the boy he never had.

I brush away my frustration while I unwrap and bite into a chocolate bar for breakfast. Dad cuts the motor, sets the boat adrift, and cracks open a beer. He takes a long sip and looks around. "Would you look at this place? Gorgeous!" he says.

Deep shades of green and the scent of the forest envelope us. The only ripples on the surface of the water are from our boat. The rest looks like glass, reflecting trees, clouds, and mountains. Few people know about this lake. Even fewer know about its coves. It's easy to believe we're the only people who have ever dared to enter this paradise.

"It's beautiful," I say. "I'm really sorry about the lure, Dad."

"Aw, it's no big deal. If I told you once, I told you a million times, if you never make any mistakes, how're you going to *learn* anything?"

"Yeah. I know." I smile weakly and tuck my candy wrapper into my jeans. I prep my pole and conservatively cast. My lure lands a safe twenty feet away from the shoreline.

"What is *that*?" he says.

"What?"

"That cast. That's not the way my Eileen casts," he says. He always calls me "my Eileen" when he's trying to teach me a lesson. "I know you see that rock right there," he says, pointing to a rock near shore. "Stop thinking about that Red Devil and put your lure next to it."

With nervous palms, I reel in my line and then cast again. The lure lands with a plop a foot from the rock. Dad smiles. "That's better," he says proudly. "Hey, a quitter never wins, and a winner never quits. Right? Never forget that, Eileen."

"I won't, Dad," I say, reeling in my line. "I won't."

5

—⟋⟍⟋—

FIVE FEET UNDER

I am waiting for Grandpa's funeral.

I'm lucky to have three sets of grandparents. I have two sets on my mom's side: Grandma and Grandpa Shelhammer take us to the Adirondacks on summer vacations, and Grandma and Grandpa Smock take us to the playground. My dad's parents, Grandma and Grandpa Gable, are Polish, first-generation Americans. They take us to the cemetery.

We are standing at my grandfather's graveside at Holy Cross Cemetery, which is on a hilltop near Scranton, Pennsylvania. We attended Mass this morning, so we're still dressed to the hilt. Dad looks uncomfortable in his tie and sport coat. Mom looks fashionable in her belted dress, complementing coat, and matching shoes. Her blonde bouffant hairstyle reminds me of a helmet worn by one of the Buckingham Palace guards.

My sisters and I are wearing dresses and pantyhose. Since I am fourteen, both my dress and my pantyhose are my mom's. There's no sense in buying me my own since I'm just about Mom's size, and her wardrobe is extensive. Mom's pantyhose sag around my ankles. I discreetly tug at the waist to keep them up. Although I dislike wearing pantyhose almost as much as I dislike wearing dresses, I'm grateful to have them on today. It's freezing up here. The March wind all too happily whips at us on the hilltop, causing my sisters and me to cross our arms and do a little shiver dance. The smell of thawing earth surrounds us as our heels sink into the ground.

Visiting a cemetery should be a solemn occasion, but I'm not sure if I should be crying, praying, or . . . giggling. After all, it's an odd thing to visit my grandfather's grave before he has passed away. It's especially odd to have him standing beside me, describing where he will be buried. I know how to talk to my other grandfathers because we have intersecting interests. But Grandpa Gable is interested in death. He sees death as a fascinating fact of life. I have no idea how to talk about that.

Although his grave is not yet marked, Grandpa has memorized its exact location. "I'm going to be buried right here," he says, holding his hands out parallel from one another like he's grasping the corners of a coffin. "Wait a minute," he adds with a confused expression. He walks to a nearby tombstone and then heads toward us again. "One, two, three, four, five, six . . . ," he says, pacing it out. "Here. It's right *here*. This is where my head is going to be," he says, pointing. "And this is where my feet are going to be."

"Uh-huh," my dad says. Out of respect, he studies the earth, purses his lips, and nods his head.

"I chose this plot because of the view. Look!" he says, pointing to the brown basin below, which has yet to show evidence of spring. "Just take a look at that valley."

I raise my eyebrows and give my grandfather a sympathetic smile. Since I am the oldest, my sisters are looking at me for clues that tell them how to react, but there is no script for this situation. Mom has on a tight, sad smile and is looking around nervously. She is softly sighing, which means she'd much rather be somewhere else. Mom is not fascinated by death; she is fascinated by life and joy and laughter. She's enduring my grandfather's morbid field trip to be polite. She looks over to Dad, who continues looking down, slowly nodding his head. I wish I knew what he was thinking.

"You should see the valley in the spring. It's beautiful," my grandfather says wistfully. He looks at me as his face breaks into a smile. My grandfather doesn't smile often, so when he does, he looks a little deranged. It scares me.

The smarty-pants teenager in me wants to tell my grandfather that he might be missing something. Namely, his life. I want to shake him and remind him that he won't be looking into the valley once he is six feet under. In fact, he won't be looking at anything. Does he realize this? Does he realize how weird it is to take your children and grandchildren to visit your final resting place before you're actually resting in it? Does he realize that most grandparents take their grandchildren to McDonald's, not to the cemetery?

———

I hold my tongue and smile at my grandfather. "You're a good girl," he says, patting my shoulder with his broad, leathered hand. "A very good girl."

I can't help but wonder if he remembers my name.

———

In spite of the fact that we inevitably end up visiting the cemetery, I love visiting my dad's parents, who eat, breathe, and live their Polish heritage. They can still speak the language and prefer Polish Mass. Because of them, I will forever love pierogies, kielbasa, polka music, and the sound of an accordion.

Whenever we visit their home, we enter through the side door. The smell of golumpki (stuffed cabbage) and percolated coffee fill the air. It's the smell of a Polish home. We immediately head into the basement where we know Grandma and Grandpa will be waiting for us. It may seem odd, but my grandparents *live* in the basement, which is the bunker of their home. It has everything they need: a full kitchen, a canning cellar, and comfy furniture. Other than their front porch, I have never seen them in any other room of their house.

My family descends the narrow staircase in rank order: Dad, Mom, me, Susie, and Mary. We take turns gripping the handrail, a painted black plumbing pipe. The linoleum steps creak as we step down. No one speaks. Silence hangs heavy in the golumpki-scented air. Since we visit only a few times a year, we're always a little nervous.

My grandparents are very, very old. Neither gets up when we

enter the room. In the far corner, Grandma is propped by pillows on her handmade daybed. Grandpa sits at attention next to her in a Queen Anne–styled upright chair.

Dad moves toward Grandma first. "Hi, Ma," he says, bending to kiss her cheek.

"Oh . . . Clarkie," my grandmother says slowly in her raspy voice. I can tell she has a special fondness for my dad, who is her ninth child out of ten. It shows in the way she says his name with tenderness, handling it gently, as she would a sparrow.

Dad extends his hand to my grandfather. "Pa," Dad says.

Grandpa looks at him sternly, as though my dad were an interloper disturbing an otherwise perfectly good evening. Finally, Grandpa's face gives way to recognition, and he accepts Dad's handshake. "Hi ya, Clarkie. Hi ya."

"Look at these girls," Grandma says, extending her pillowy arms to us. My sisters and I take turns sinking into her embrace. We kiss her powdery cheeks; her white, curly hair brushes against our faces. We move toward Grandpa and offer him a quick kiss. We take our places, quietly waiting behind Dad, ready to follow his lead. Mom does the same.

"How ya doin', Pa?" my dad asks.

Grandpa shoots him a harsh look and shouts his standard reply: "I'm five feet under!" He means he is just one foot shy of being dead and buried *six* feet under—in his much-considered grave. If Grandpa had a sense of humor, an answer like that would spark some good-natured teasing. But Grandpa had worked in the coal mines since he was nine years old. When you get your education from the depths of the earth, it's hard to find the light.

Grandpa begins to recite his ailments, along with the ailments of everyone he knows. Every disease is emphasized with the word *the,* as in "Jimmy Czarnecki has the diabetes" . . . "Mary Gorski has the arthritis" . . . "Sam Duda has the prostate cancer." From the sound of it, I'm pretty sure Grandpa and most of his friends could die any minute. I'm not the only one who believes this. Margie, my closest cousin, who is also fourteen, tells me Grandpa announces regularly, "We are all born to die!" without warning. We're all a little terrified of him.

"Ach! Don't listen to him," Grandma says, waving her hand dismissively. She turns to my mom and says, "Bonnie, get the girls something to drink. You girls want some birch beer?"

My sisters and I perk up. Birch beer is a little like root beer with a lot more kick in the pants. We only drink it when we visit Dad's family. Even if we *could* buy birch beer in New York, we wouldn't. We want to preserve its specialness.

Mom collects four small juice glasses from the white metal cupboards. She opens the old-style fridge and pulls out a beer for Dad and a large glass bottle of birch beer for us. Dad breaks open the beer and stares at the ceiling as he takes a long sip. My sisters and I sip our sodas like champagne.

In my grandparents' home, children may speak only when spoken to, so my sisters and I listen silently to the stilted conversation. Although we want to run outside and climb down the steep, rocky hill in back of our grandparents' home, we're also content to sit, listen, and look around the basement a while. There's something pathetically beautiful about it all.

I try to imagine what it might have been like to grow up here.

Raising ten children should have guaranteed raucous meals filled with the clatter of young, exciting lives, but meals were sacred in this home. When my dad was growing up, three rules governed mealtimes: No one missed dinner. No one took more food than he or she could eat. And no one, under any circumstances, was allowed to talk.

It's hard to picture a family of twelve eating dinner night after night like Benedictine monks. But Grandpa wouldn't tolerate noise or disturbances of any kind. No laughter. No arguments. No stories. In addition, everyone at the table was expected to intuitively know what Grandpa wanted at the exact moment he wanted it. Silence heightened everyone's radar. For instance, they were expected to guess the exact moment he would want to drink his coffee. And if the family did not immediately pass down the accompaniments, he would give them "the look" and then bellow, "Can't you see I'm ready for the cream and sugar?!" The tension alone could destroy the most voracious appetites.

My sisters and I continue to listen to the adult conversation. Grandpa shifts into his coal-mining stories as we sip the last of our birch beer. Once Mom determines that we've waited a respectable amount of time, she lets us go. We walk as quietly as possible toward the narrow stairs. I look back to see my grandmother's gnarled hands clasped in the lap of her flowered housecoat. Her fleshy arms press against her smooshed bosom. She watches us leave the room with a delighted look on her face. Her expression reminds me of my dad's. I glance at my grandfather, who watches us with stern curiosity. His expression reminds me of the army sergeant he once was. I resolve to keep out of trouble.

A photograph of my grandparents on their wedding day hangs near the front door. My grandfather is standing at attention in his army uniform. Beside him is my equally serious grandmother, a short and skinny bride. I stare into their young eyes, searching them for love and romance. I find neither. Instead, they stare back at me soberly, as if readying themselves for treacherous roads ahead.

They were right to be solemn. Grandpa served in World War I. He and Grandma survived the Depression in spite of having ten ravenous mouths to feed. When coal miners would strike, demanding better wages and working conditions, Grandpa would tell the family, "It's time to tighten our belts!" Everyone thought, *Good grief! What's left to tighten?*

They kept alive by raising chickens, gardening, and canning anything they could stuff into a mason jar. They also survived because Harry Waldman, a Jewish grocer whom my grandmother always accused of trying to cheat her, allowed them to purchase things on credit. Over the years, the Waldman's grocery tab amounted to over a thousand dollars, a colossal amount of money in the early fifties. Once my dad was on his own, he proudly paid it off.

Since there was never any money, my dad and his siblings were not allowed to ask for anything. Grandpa would go bananas if they asked for the car, a few bucks, or permission to join the track team. When they were children, my aunts and uncles once summoned up enough courage to ask for a sled.

"What do you want to do, kill yourselves?!" my grandfather roared. They never asked again.

———

—⁓—

Twice a year my family visits my grandparents' waiting place for the weekend. Time passes slowly here, and laughter is in short supply. As much as I enjoy visiting them, I'm always a little grateful to leave. It's difficult for a kid to remember to be quiet, keep out of trouble, and behave for three whole days in a row. After a weekend of coal-mining stories, cancer revelations, and cemetery visits, it feels good to drive back toward life.

It is four o'clock Sunday afternoon, and we are descending into my grandparents' basement once again, this time to say good-bye. Unfortunately, we have arrived during my grandfather's dinnertime, so we'll have to rush our departure so he can eat in peace. "We'll see ya, Pa," Dad says.

Grandpa sits alone and upright at the end of the table. Before him is a steaming plate full of chicken, peas, potatoes, and gravy, all made by Aunt Leona, who lives next door. My sisters and I dutifully move toward Grandpa to kiss him good-bye. He sits unyielding, his eyes flashing with fury, and says nothing. He doesn't have to. My dad knows "the look" that screams, *Can't you see that I'm eating?!*

My sisters and I quickly peck him on his scratchy cheek. Grandpa remains silent. There are no returned kisses, no "Thanks for comings" or "Great to see yous." He sits erect at the head of the table, where he eats alone. A paper napkin is tucked haphazardly into the top of his shirt. His right hand grasps a fork, holding it upright. His left hand is clenched in a fist. He is eating, gosh darn it. *Eating!* He is a lion hovering over his prey, ready to defend his meal.

Dad doesn't bother to shake his father's hand. Mom clears her throat. "Bye, Pa," she says, gently. Grandpa says nothing in response. We back out of the room, climb the stairs, swing open the storm door, and leave. Our family piles into the car and drives away. Dad's seething anger silently oozes from him, filling the car with the same kind of tension he was raised with. He cannot believe his father is still more interested in his dinner than in his own family.

Dad quietly but resolutely resolves that we will not return.

—◈—

Grandma died three years after that visit at the age of eighty-six. Grandpa died six years later at the age of ninety-four. As I drive across the Pennsylvania border on my way to his funeral, I think about how he chose to live. Throughout my entire childhood and young adulthood, Grandpa waited to die. I can't help but wonder how his life and relationships might have been different had he chosen to live.

During Grandpa's calling hours and viewing in the wall-papered funeral home chapel, I am surrounded by cousins, aunts, and uncles. Even though I only see them at weddings and funerals, I love these polka-dancing people. We hug and kiss. I listen, rapt, loving the way they chew their words when they talk about their gallbladders and colonoscopies. They tell me I've grown into a beautiful young lady and ask me about my college major. When I tell them it's communication, Uncle Joe brightens. "Ah, you're going to be the next Barbara Walters!" Aunt Leona tells me there's no money in television. She says I should switch my major and become a nurse instead.

The next day our extensive family huddles around Grandpa's gravesite, trying to keep warm under the green funeral canopy in the frigid December winds. The frozen earth is hard under our feet. The air smells like snow and my aunts' perfume. Grandpa's dark wooden casket is blanketed with red roses. I stand between my dad and sisters. Dad is wearing his black and gray funeral suit. Since my sisters and I are now grown, the dresses and pantyhose we wear are our own.

The priest finishes his prayers and final blessings "in the name of the Father, the Son, and the Holy Spirit," gesticulating the sign of the cross in the air. Before my grandfather's casket is lowered into the ground, someone sings a short song in Polish, the same one Grandpa had belted out at many gravesides over the years. The song is achingly poignant, and it makes my father cry.

Grandpa's wait is finally over.

My sisters and I lower our heads and listen as everyone whispers their final good-byes to the family's stern patriarch. This time around, we don't have to look imploringly at one another, hoping to glimpse clues about how to act. Grandpa is not standing beside us, telling us where his head and feet will rest. We're old enough now to know that death is an integral part of life. We no longer have to imagine it; we can see it with our own eyes.

I look over my shoulder and peer into the valley, the same one Grandpa pointed out to me many years ago. It looks gray and sad, like death itself. Soon it will be blanketed by Old Man Winter. A few months from now, winter will give way to spring, and the valley will burst with new life. Although I know better, I find myself hoping that Grandpa enjoys the view.

6

H-E-A-R-T (EIGHT POINTS)

I am waiting for my gram to spell a word.

I have shuffled around my Scrabble letters and can hardly wait to spell the most perfect word: *phony*. I will use the *O* in *valor*, which I already spelled out a few turns before, earning eighteen points. *Phony* will award me thirty-eight points since the *P* will land on a triple-letter-score square, and the *Y* will land on a double-word-score square.

I am sweating in anticipation of such a prize although I shouldn't be as excited as I am. I already know I will win the game. I almost always win when I play Scrabble against my grandma, so winning comes cheap. Deep down I know that spending time with my grandmother is what is important, but my competitiveness rears its ugly head in the stupidest places. Playing a benign game of Scrabble is one of the few things she and I do together and is about as action-packed as our times together get. And so I wait.

"I have the worst letters," Grandma says, which is what she always says when we play Scrabble. "I can't spell a thing."

"I hate bad letters," I say. "Do you have any vowels?"

"Yeah."

"Consonants?"

"Yeah."

"Do you have the *Q*? I hate being stuck with the *Q*."

"Not yet. I'll probably pull that next since I don't have a *U* either," she says. She sighs and shrugs, scowling at the letters before her.

She moves her letters around, hoping a word might suddenly appear before her. While she does this, I watch her hands. I have always loved my grandmother's hands. They are small, thin, spotted, and papery. They are also plagued by arthritis and age, so she moves them slowly and shakily.

She keeps her nails trimmed because hers are busy hands; they're not for show. Most of all, I love the blue veins that run through the backs of her hands. I don't know anything about reading palms, but if I were a palm reader and my grandmother walked into my den to have her palms read, I imagine I would turn her palms over and read the backs of her hands instead. There you can read the secrets to her life, mapped in blue. All the work. All the struggle. All the pain. All the quiet beauty. Drawn clearly for the entire world to see.

"I love your hands, Gram," I say absentmindedly.

"What?" she says, and she looks at me sharply as though I have just said something deeply offensive to her. "They're ugly."

Like a child who has been caught doing something naughty, she hides her hands under the table where I can't see them. She's a little angry. She either believes I am just trying to be nice or thinks I am flat-out lying. I can tell that she suddenly doesn't trust me. Not with Scrabble. Certainly not as a judge of beauty. My comment has managed to erase the quiet comfort of the moment.

"I'm sorry, Gram. It's just that I really love your hands. I've always loved your hands. When I'm your age, I hope my hands are just like yours."

"Humph," she grunts. "Don't say that. You don't want hands like mine. You just need to stop biting your nails, Eileen, that's all. Then you'll have pretty hands."

Now I'm the one who is self-conscious. I hide my own stubby fingers beneath the table. Biting my nails is a habit I cannot seem to break. I sucked my thumb as a baby until my mother bought that awful cayenne-pepper stuff and brushed it over my thumbs, which made me howl and beg for water whenever I placed them idly in my mouth. (I know this from overhearing Mom advise friends and relatives over the years on how to break their own kids of the habit.)

Years later, she brushed that same evil stuff over my preteen nails and then painted my mind with potent images, determined to break me of my habit. "Do you know the kind of germs that linger under your fingernails, Eileen? They're the worst kind. Worse than toilet germs. And you're putting all of them into your mouth!" she said.

————

The images grossed me out, but only for a while. Within hours, I had washed off the pepper juice and shoved my spicy stubs into my mouth once again.

My mother is my grandmother's daughter. To say she's meticulous about her own nails is a huge understatement. She spends several hours a week filing, clipping, and polishing them. Sometimes she drinks a mysterious daily gelatin mixture that's supposed to strengthen them and help them grow even longer. Her Avon lady keeps her well supplied with a rainbow of colors. Mom would love to share her nail-polish collection with me, if only my stubs deserved such a privilege.

Now, as I wait for Grandma to spell a word, I absentmindedly stick one of my fingers in my mouth.

"Eileen, you're biting."

"Sorry. I just can't help it."

I want to make her proud of me, and for the most part, I do. This one habit comes between us, and I tell myself to try a little harder because I know it will make her happy. Some years, I give up biting my nails for Lent. It's amazing, really, how quickly nails grow when given the chance. Three weeks into Lent, I have little white bands on the tips of my fingers that can legitimately be called "nails." Whenever this happens, I proudly extend my hands to my grandma each time I visit. "Just *look* at your nice hands, Eileen. Beautiful," she says, admiring them as she gently holds my hands in her own.

But then Lent ends, and something makes me nervous or makes me think extra hard, and my silly promise to God that I won't bite my nails is quickly forgotten. My nails find their way back to my mouth so I can chew them into oblivion.

Once in a while, when I'm bored at Grandma's house (which is an easy thing to be), I ask her if I can go into her bedroom and use her nail file. She always says yes, and my heart does a little dance at the chance to enter her secret place.

Grandma keeps her bedroom door closed because she doesn't want nosy somebodies like my sisters and me looking at her stuff. Her bedroom is the darkest, quietest place in her house. The air is lighter, and a hush blankets the space. I turn the glass doorknob (which I love enough to steal if I could get away with it) and open the door so quietly you would think I was trying not to wake someone. In fact, I don't want to disturb this intimate space. I want to move slowly enough to enjoy my visit there.

Like the rest of her house, the room is tiny. It manages to fit only a full-size bed, dresser, night table, and sewing machine. Her bed is covered with a blue chenille bedspread and is always neatly made. Everything, from her housecoat to her hatboxes, has a place—and is in it.

A single picture, measuring eight by ten, adorns the wall. It's a picture of a black and white puppy with an extra-large head and enormous, sad black eyes, standing on the surface of the moon. He looks lonely, and the tilt of his head begs me to save him. Instead, I think I might just want to give Gram a new picture.

My mother tried to do that a few times over the years. In the seventies, she went through a plaster of paris phase, and she floated a picture of Jesus' face in a flat plaster mold. I thought the finished plaque was beautiful. I loved seeing Jesus' innocent, blue-eyed, tanned face surrounded with all that white stuff. But my grandmother didn't seem to like it very much, and I never did see the plaster of paris Jesus again.

While in Grandma's bedroom, I reach for the nail file, which is always waiting in the exact same place on her dresser. I like the predictability of knowing where her things are, even if most of them are private things. She never changes any of them, and it's a relief from my family's home, which is in utter chaos most of the time. My sisters and I are grateful if we can find a working hair dryer or a box of Lucky Charms that still has a few marshmallows in it. At Grandma's house, nothing seems to run out. Everything has its place. Everything has a purpose. Decorations are few. Dust is wiped away. The nail file is always next to the nail clippers, which are next to the brush with the bristles facing downward, which is next to the light-blue plastic mirror Grandma uses to see the back of her hair to make sure there are no "holes" between brushed-out curls. It's the way it is.

I grab the nail file and peek into the mirror over her dresser, giving it a different face to reflect back. I take a deep breath, like I always do in my grandmother's room, because the air is different. It smells like Grandma, like lavender talcum powder and clean pantyhose.

If I don't leave quickly enough, Grandma will call out, "Did you find it?" She loves me, but she's a private lady who doesn't want anyone rummaging around in her stuff. It should only take a few seconds to find the nail file anyway. Like I said, it's always in the same place.

"I think I'm going to have to pass," Grandma says now, bringing me back to the Scrabble game in front of me. "My letters really are awful."

"Here, let me see if I can help," I say, and she turns the letters around to me. The fact that she actually has very good letters makes me feel sad. Scrabble has become more difficult for her in recent years. I long for it to be the way it was in years past. I want her to beat me because she has spelled the word *money* on a triple-word-score square or has figured out how to use her *S* and spell *switch* on a big, fat word that was already played.

I no longer want to play Scrabble with my grandma because it reminds me that her faculties are diminishing and that one day she will die and leave me forever. This last fact is what compels me to return to her tiny house and play Scrabble over and over again.

I don't come often enough. (She'd like to see me a few times a week.) When I do show up, I don't stay as long as she'd like. (She'd have me spend a whole afternoon.) I have to press down my energies when I'm in her presence because I'm apt to run circles around her. I am young and full of life. I'm busy. I'm in college, after all. I have a boyfriend who needs attention. Plus, I'm a leader at the college, and I have responsibilities. I have homework and a few jobs.

The impatient part of me is thinking, *Look, Gram, I don't have time for this. I'm on my own, you know. Do you realize how nice it is of me to sit here in your itsy-bitsy kitchen playing this dumb game of Scrabble even though I would rather be doing something else? Anything else, really. Like running. Or working. Or spending time with my boyfriend whose energy matches my own (or exceeds it, if you know what I mean). Or laughing with friends. Or sleeping. Because I'm tired, oh-so-tired, and I need some rest because I'm going, going, going all the time.*

But I tell her none of this, and I stuff my frustrations deep into my gut. In the back of my mind, I know something I don't want to admit. I know there will come a day, not too many years from now, when I will enter my grandmother's room at the nursing home, and she will no longer recognize me. She'll give me her cute little smile and say, "Well, hi!" like she always does. She'll turn to the nurse who has just settled her into her wheelchair and introduce me by saying, "This is my niece." And, in that moment, my heart will break.

I also know there will come a day, at the end of her life, when I will be met with an orange banner that has been posted across her nursing room door, warning those who want to enter that this is not an ordinary day for Edna Smock. On this day, her life—her beautiful, simple, quiet, confused life—has ended, and all those who want to visit will need to understand that, while her body lies still in the bed, she is no longer there.

And on that day, I will be the first of her family members to arrive. I'll stop at her door and turn back to the front desk to ask about the banner even though I already know the answer in my heart: my grandmother has passed away. She died alone. Once my fears are confirmed, I'll duck under the banner and close the door behind me. I'll walk over to her bed, and I'll look into her sweet face with her glassy eyes half open and her jaw that has gone slack. And I'll cry. I'll cry with a grief that I didn't know was in me. I'll try to close her eyes and mouth because I know she wouldn't want people looking at her like that. And I'll say, "I'm sorry, Grandma. Oh, I'm so sorry," over and over and over again.

Finally, I'll take her cold hands into my own, and I will hold them. She can't pull them away from me or tell me they're ugly. I'll study them until I've memorized them and their likeness is pressed into my being. Even more than her lovely face, it will be her hands that I will carry around in my memory. It is their intimacy I will treasure for the rest of my own days. In the years that follow her death, I will imitate her life with my own hands. I'll learn how to make her pickles, applesauce, and jams. I'll learn how to garden and find joy in the yield of well-tended beds. I'll hang my wash on the line and watch, with surprising pleasure, my sheets dance in the sun. I'll read books from the library by the dozens while holding them like presents in my own arthritic hands.

I'll watch the map on the back of my hands turn from simple country roads into mangled city streets. I'll play Scrabble with my own energetic granddaughter. And when she tells me, "I love your hands, Grandma," I won't hide them. Instead, I'll stretch them across the table and show her the gnarled mess of my stubs and say, "I know. Aren't they beautiful? They look just like *my* grandma's."

But all that won't happen for many, many years. Right now, I'm still waiting for my grandma—my lovely, short, quiet grandma—to spell a word with her "awful" letters: *T, N, I, S, I, T,* and *J.*

"Hm. Well, you could spell *joist*," I say, pointing to the *O* on the board, the very same *O* I planned on using for *phony*. The resulting word gives her twenty-four points, fourteen points less than what I would have gotten for *phony*. I've handicapped myself, but it's the right thing to do. After all, she's my gram.

"Whew. Okay, your turn," she says as she reaches into the bag that holds fewer and fewer letters. "Ugh! I just can't believe it!"

I know at that moment that she has managed to pull out the *Q*, so I quickly scan the board and realize there's an empty *U* waiting for her. I resolve to leave the area around it alone. Since

Grandma's *joist* has taken my *phony*, I'm at a momentary loss as to what to do.

"Is it my turn?" Grandma says.

"Nope. Still mine," I say, feeling slightly pressured.

"Bad letters, huh?"

"Yeah."

"I've had bad letters all day," she says.

"Yeah. Me, too. I hate that," I say.

"So do I."

She looks around her tiny kitchen, and I can tell she is tired of waiting for me because she has figured out a way to dump her *Q*. I hastily throw my *H* next to an empty *I*: *hi*. That's the best I can do under the circumstances.

"Just five points, huh?" she says.

"Yeah. It's okay. I'll get you the next turn," I say playfully.

With slightly shaky fingers she picks up her *Q* and places it next to the *U*. With back-and-forth motions, she adds an *I* and a *T*.

"*Quit*," she says. She's extra proud that her *Q* has landed on the double-letter-score square. It's given her twenty-three points.

"Aw, man," I say, feigning disappointment. "Awesome, Gram!"

"I'm just glad I wasn't stuck with it. I hate that *Q*."

"Me, too."

I look up from the board and smile into her face as I tuck my secret into my heart—one I'll pull out later and smile at, when Scrabble with Gram is no longer possible. The entire time she spelled I had watched her hands.

7

Love Is . . .

I am waiting for a sign.

I am a senior at Roberts Wesleyan College, in love with a guy named Brad Button. I have always wanted to date a Brad because I love the name, and every Brad I have ever known has been beautiful. As for his last name, Button, well . . . it's just cute.

I ask him if anyone teases him about his name or if they tell him he is "as cute as a button." He says no one does. Most likely, it's due to his size and demeanor. Brad personifies "tall, dark, and handsome." He's a six-foot-six, lean, muscular basketball-playing machine. He has straight, dark hair, broad shoulders, and piercing blue eyes. He is quiet, thoughtful, and smart. Until a year ago he thought he wanted to become a corporate executive, but that was before God stepped into the picture and rearranged the furniture. He now believes God has some kind of call on his life for ministry. Neither one of us knows what to do with that. So we hang out, run together on the coed college track team, make out in the late evening, and pray for direction.

I am beginning to believe that God has some kind of call on my life, too. Until recently I had big plans to move to Florida after graduation and get a job promoting Disney World. I have ended past relationships because I knew that Disney, not marriage, was my destiny. But that was before Brad stepped into the picture and rearranged *my* furniture. Now I can't imagine a future without Brad in it. And that scares me to death.

My fear is not understood by the many girls at my Christian liberal arts college who are more interested in obtaining their MRS degree than their bachelor's. Since I am more Gloria Steinem than Betty Crocker, I can't wrap my brain around this thinking. Even more confusing to me are the girls who announce that God is calling them to become pastors' wives. Why, I wonder, would God call anyone to become the spouse of someone else's occupation?

Anyhow, I have no intention of one day walking across the stage to accept my college diploma and the next day walking down the aisle. I'm young. I'm independent. I don't believe I need a man in order to be complete in God's eyes or my own. But I also love and want Brad. And that's a problem.

I think other people know that this relationship is for keeps. They boldly ask me when Brad and I are going to get engaged. "Get outta here," I tell them as I change the topic. But I can't blow off everyone.

———

My Scrabble-playing grandma, for instance, fell in love with Brad the moment she met him. She regularly sends me letters in which she details weather patterns and sends me obituary notices and newspaper articles. Most of the time, she includes one or two clippings from the comic strip titled *Love is . . .* that features two doe-eyed, cherub-looking characters, one boy and one girl. The comic strip might read, "Love is . . . snuggling." Or, "Love is . . . holding hands." My gram wants me to be happy. Even though she's been divorced and remarried, she still believes my happiness lies with the right guy.

Less than one month after Brad and I began dating, she sent me this letter:

June 9, 1987
Dear Eileen,

After meeting Brad, I feel I can quit worrying about you. I can't help but feel he's the one you may settle down and be happy with. We liked him very much. Just the fact that you wanted us all to meet him told me how proud you are of him. How did you manage to overlook him for so long? Are you in any of his classes or just track? With his long legs, he's sure a winner.

We love you,
Grandma

P.S. I like Brad's dimples, too, when he smiles.

She enclosed a comic panel that read, "Love is . . . making him part of your future." *After only one month? Jeez, Gram.* Still, I couldn't help but think she might be on to something. Doesn't Grandma always know best?

—⚬—

Throughout our senior year, Brad and I pray about our future. We ask God about his plan for our lives, hoping he might give us a sign. Carefully, we discuss marriage. We both know it is a huge step. When we marry, we want to marry for keeps. I've experienced firsthand the devastating effects that divorce has on a family, and I want nothing to do with that ever, *ever* again.

In the first semester the pressure mounts in both the career and relationship departments. This seems tragically unfair. How can twenty-two-year-olds be expected to make decisions that will impact the rest of their lives? Still, we know that 1 Corinthians 7:9 says, "It is better to marry than to burn with passion," and Brad and I are on fire. He's so beautiful. There's this sweet spot where his neck meets his shoulders that I adore. I can't imagine graduating, getting my own apartment, and behaving myself when he comes over, especially with that sexy clavicle of his. I want him by my side day and night. I also want the timing to be right.

Now Brad and I are driving the last half mile toward the college. I am sitting in the front seat of Brad's car, an orange 1974 Plymouth Volare, which he calls Betsy. The inside smells like old people; Betsy shakes and shudders whenever she goes over fifty miles an hour. She's ancient and rusty, but we love Betsy because her bench seats make it possible for me to sit right next to Brad while he drives. She's cozy.

It is December 21. Our last exam is tomorrow. We should be studying instead of riding around in Betsy, but it's too magical a night to be holed up in the library. After dinner in the campus cafeteria, we go out for ice cream, and now we're heading back to campus. Betsy's headlights illuminate the snow that falls heavily, guaranteeing a white Christmas. We look at the lights that people have strung around the perimeters of their houses and bushes.

"I want you to know something, Brad," I say, with my body pressed against his side, my hand on his knee.

"Yeah?"

"Well, I've been praying about, you know, whether we should get married or not. And I want you to know, I'm going to relax about the whole thing."

"Really?"

"Yeah. I was praying about it this morning. I've really been waiting for a sign. And I just think that God will tell us when the time is right. I'm not going to worry about it anymore. I have a peace about it."

"Huh. Well . . . good."

"I know. I've been really wound up about it, but I'm not going to be that way anymore. We'll know."

"I agree," he says. "Hey, do you want to go to the church to pray?"

We really have to study for tomorrow's final, but prayer is important. More important than studying. "Sure."

Brad unlocks one of the doors to the campus church, and we slip inside the dark lobby. We probably shouldn't be here, but Brad is an usher and has been trusted with master keys. It's a privilege we don't take for granted. It's cool to be in this empty, sacred space on a weeknight evening instead of a crowded Sunday morning.

"I gotta go potty," I say.

"Okay," Brad says, chuckling. If he wanted someone who was überfeminine, he picked the wrong girlfriend. "I'll be inside the sanctuary."

I finish my business and wash my hands, catching my reflection in the bathroom mirror. I am a lucky girl. Correction: I am a *blessed* girl. (Christians, I've learned, don't believe in luck.) I might be on the brink of full-blown adulthood, but I'm ready for whatever my unknown future throws at me. I have a good education, a loving boyfriend, and a strong personal faith. Those are good things to grow a future on. I dry my hands on a paper towel, walk through the dark lobby, and open the doors to the sanctuary.

Before me is a sight so lovely it catches my breath. I find myself wishing I had a camera, but it couldn't possibly capture the moment. Brad kneels at the altar, a single spotlight illuminating him. The rest of the sanctuary, which normally seats eight hundred, is completely dark, so Brad looks especially holy to me. I quietly make my way up the aisle and kneel next to him, noticing a single pink rose and a Bible on the red carpet in front of us.

"Aw," I say. "Hey."

"Hey," he says, leaning into me for a gentle kiss. "How are you doing?" The tears that fill his eyes tell me this is probably not going to be an ordinary night.

"Uh. How're *you* doing?" I ask a little nervously.

"Well," he says. He swallows, nudges my shoulder with his, and looks into my eyes. "I committed my life to Christ at this altar over a year ago. I think it's time I made my next commitment."

He reaches into his pocket, pulls out a little blue velvet box, and reveals a sweet, pear-shaped diamond. "I love you, Eileen. Will you marry me?"

Oh, my word! This is it. This is really it. I want to press the Pause button on this moment so I can stand up and look around. I want to remember the exact slant of the spotlight as it shines down on us, the earnest look on Brad's young face, the feel of my body, kneeling on the carpeted altar.

"Yes!" I say, without hesitation. We are young and naive. We don't yet have our degrees or jobs or medical benefits. But we have each other. And we share a passion for God. What more do we really need?

He slips the ring on my finger. It fits perfectly. "I'd like to base our future on Psalm 91," he says, reaching for the Bible.

"Okay."

He flips through the pages and begins reading aloud. "He who dwells in the secret place of the Most High shall abide under the shadow of the Almighty. I will say of the LORD, 'He is my refuge and my fortress; my God, in Him I will trust.'"

The psalm is chock-full of adventure, danger, and darkness but promises that God will protect through it all. In the sixteenth verse, it ends with, "With long life I will satisfy him, and show him My salvation."

It sounds like a good plan: an exciting, risk-filled life; God's protection through calamity; and a long life together. What more could we ask for?

———

Brad arrives back at his dorm room late at night to find that our friend Steve has slipped something under his door. It's a note of congratulations and a calligraphy copy of Psalm 91. Steve had no idea that Brad planned to use the psalm when he asked me to marry him. Brad and I interpret it as a sign from God.

—⁓—

September is a beautiful month for a wedding. It's raining on our day, but it doesn't faze me. Nothing could rob me of my excitement. Grasping my father's arm, I walk down the aisle toward Brad and our unknown future together.

I am wearing a three-hundred-dollar wedding gown that I bought off the rack. It's pretty (in an eighties kinda way) with a tight bodice, poufy sleeves, and an extra-long train that requires lots of fussing from my six bridesmaids. The dress is much too long for me, so I'm wearing white three-inch Kmart heels that are killing my feet. I'm also wearing my mom's poufy crinoline slip, hoping it will push the skirt out enough to keep me from tripping on it. The slip is too big for me, so I taped it to my chest with masking tape. My tape job is not pretty, but hey, who's going to see it?

There are seven steps at the front of the church that give the wedding tableau an extra-regal look. My train will spill down the stairs just like Princess Diana's did on her wedding day. While dressing, my bridesmaids talk about how they hope they won't trip on the stairs. "Don't worry," I say. "You're not going to trip. No one ever trips. You'll be fine." I'm not concerned at all about this nonproblem; my days as a gymnast have prepared me to balance on just about anything.

—⁂—

"Who gives this woman to this man in marriage?" the pastor asks.

"Her mother and I do," my dad says. He turns to face me, lifts the blusher veil away from my face, and kisses and hugs me before taking his seat next to my mom. I join Brad at the foot of the stairs, and we begin to climb them together. I hear a dreaded *psft!* sound as I accidentally step on my too-long slip and the tape rips away from my chest. Once we get to the top, I feel the slip settling dangerously downward. When it's time to light the unity candle, I literally have to kick it away from my legs to move forward. *Note to self,* I think. *Next time you tape undergarments to your chest, use duct tape instead of masking tape.*

Still, no one knows that my slip is a free agent, and I'm a good faker. As the ceremony comes to a close, I know that all I have to do is get down the steps and walk back down the aisle. I can do this. I take Brad's arm with my left hand and reach down to gather my too-long skirt and unattached too-long slip with my right. I'm certain I've grabbed both, but I'm mistaken. I step directly onto the sagging slip, lose my balance, and fall into my new husband while three hundred people simultaneously gasp. Out of the corner of my eye, I see my dad leap out of the pew with outstretched arms. He's fifteen feet and seven stair-steps away, but gosh darn it, he's gonna catch his daughter. When Brad catches and steadies me instead, Dad slumps back into the pew with a "Whew!"

"It *happens!*" I say aloud to our friends and family.

As the congregation laughs, Brad leans into me. "What's going on, babe?"

"My slip fell off," I whisper back.

And so Brad and I stumble, literally and figuratively, into our life together.

—⟋∿⟍—

There are those who linger in the waiting place their entire lives, hoping for love that never seems to find them. There are those who gamble away their entire futures on the first relationship to come along. Then there are those of us who are fortunate enough to find The One.

No love is perfect. But who wants perfect love? Perfect love would not accompany heartache, struggle, or sorrow, and without those things we'd never be able to understand love's strength. No one *really* understands love's capacities until everyday life whups it around just to see what it's made of.

I think my gram was right: "Love is . . . making him a part of your future." It's also catching each other when we stumble, saying yes to one another's dreams (even at the expense of our own), and surviving the mundane even when it threatens to kill you. Love is . . . full of adventure, danger, and darkness. Love is . . . always worth waiting for.

8

—ᴍ—

LESSONS IN HUMILITY

I am waiting for my dignity to return.

The waiting room of the South Philadelphia WIC (Women, Infants, and Children) office is dreary and desperate-feeling. But here I sit, seven months pregnant with our second child, waiting for a state employee to call my name.

I really don't belong in this place. After all, Brad and I have master's degrees, and we work our buns off. Brad works seventy-plus hours a week starting a brand-new church in Center City, Philadelphia, and I work on contract as a corporate trainer while caring for two-and-a-half-year-old Stephen. We do the best we can, but we are barely making it. Our combined income is low enough to meet the WIC requirements for a family of (almost) four. We are living out Brad's dream for ministry but learning that dreams often don't pay very well. We can use whatever help we can get.

Brad should probably be at my side, but applying to WIC is not his idea. It's mine. After all, I'm the one who gathers the food, manages our finances, and pays the bills. I'm the one who figures out how to make it when there's too much month left at the end of the money. I'm the one who has the time. Brad relented to the idea as long as he didn't have to do it. I can't blame him, really. This place is a hole. But the WIC groceries will help our family, so I'm willing to swallow my pride, fill out the paperwork, produce the necessary documents, and sit here until my name is called.

The waiting room is deeply depressing. The smell of dirty diapers and body odor weaves itself through the unconditioned air. The thin, brown carpet is stained with formula, apple juice, and Lord only knows what else. Mismatched plastic chairs surround a sticky coffee table. There are no windows or magazines. A few donated plastic toys are scattered across the gross floor. A two-year-old with long, thick lashes plays with a toy on the coffee table. With great concentration, he moves a wooden bead up and down, up and down a colorful wire. His left nostril is crusted with snot, and he repeatedly blows a green bubble from it. I want to wipe it away and clean up his face, but his mom is sitting just three seats away with her arms and legs crossed, staring at a dirty white wall. So I just sit here, too, watching her son's snot bubble blowing and popping, blowing and popping.

I'm not easily nauseated, but the scene around me turns my

stomach. I'm positive no one bothers to disinfect the toys for these children. If this were Gymboree, the toys would be cleaned and sterilized daily, but this ain't no Gymboree. This is the South Philly WIC office. The two places are as different as a Donald Trump mansion and a Jeff Foxworthy redneck trailer.

"Come here, Stephen. Come sit on my lap," I say, wanting to protect my son from this place and snot-bubble boy.

Stephen ignores my attempt to de-germify him and continues exploring the room. He has enough curiosity and energy for three children. "Mama, look!" he says, holding up a wooden dinosaur puzzle with three missing pieces.

"What is that?"

"A dye-a-saur!" he says, dumping the pieces onto the skanky floor. He plops his diapered bottom next to a stain and begins putting the puzzle together. "Rrraaarrr!" he says.

I try not to think of the number of children who have sucked on the puzzle pieces before Stephen has had the chance to handle them. I wish I could have left him home with Brad, but I was told to bring him to every appointment. After Kristina is born, I will need to bring her, too. Thinking about bringing a baby into this place makes me shudder.

Employees say they need the children present so they can check their hemoglobin levels. I know they also inspect them for signs of malnutrition or abuse. This last fact nauseates me and almost kept me from moving forward with this plan. Almost. I decided to come anyway because free food will make our months easier. As I shift uneasily in my seat, I remind myself that God doesn't appreciate a pride-filled heart. Pride comes before a fall, right? Still, I gather my courage and try to sit taller. There is no sense in hanging my head in shame.

The ten-by-ten waiting room is filled with five moms, seven children, and two infants. Two children are fighting over a Tupperware shape-sorter toy. When the red and blue plastic sides close on the fingers of one little boy, he lets out a soul-piercing wail. His mother grabs him by the left arm and jerks him over to her. "You's all right," she says meanly into his face. "Quit that cryin'." He wails louder.

"He's beautiful," I say, attempting to diffuse the situation.

"Yeah? You wan 'im?" she says with raised eyebrows.

I smile sympathetically. "He's just really, really beautiful."

A tall woman wearing a beige and white tropical-patterned dress enters the room. "Button!" she says.

"That's us, Stephen. Come with me, baby," I say, relieved to get out of the miserable waiting room.

Martha leads me to her office and tells me to have a seat. I take Stephen into my lap, even though space between my waist and my knees has become a nonexistent commodity since my huge belly now occupies much of my thighs. Martha takes a seat with her back to two dirty, curtainless windows. Since there's no air-conditioning in this place, I'm sure she hopes to catch an occasional breeze.

She opens my paperwork and reviews my application. "So . . . you're married?" she says.

"Yes."

"And your husband? He's employed?"

"Yes. He's a pastor," I say, as if that explains my presence here.

Martha is nice and seems to understand. She's used to having people scam the system, so naturally she's suspicious of a married woman with a master's degree who is attempting to obtain WIC checks in South Philadelphia. It doesn't seem to add up.

—⁓—

Relieved, I walk out of the WIC office with a handful of checks that will help us obtain free food. It's amazing. Wonderful, really. I do the math and figure it will provide the equivalent of forty dollars a month, and forty extra dollars will make a huge difference in our food budget. My heart is filled with gratitude as I walk to the nearest grocery store with Stephen in his stroller.

I walk the aisles, using the checks as my grocery list, and collect gallons of milk, bags of grated cheese, peanut butter, Cheerios, and a one-pound bag of pinto beans (even though I have no clue what to do with dry beans). At the checkout, I place my WIC checks on the conveyor belt in front of the items. I'm excited about the free food, but I'm also nervous, as though I'm doing something wrong. *This is no big deal, Eileen. Stand tall. Do it for your family.*

I watch the checks move forward on the belt and try to get the attention of the cashier whose name tag reads "May I help you Sandy." I watch helplessly as the pile of checks reach the thin metal bar. Just as I make a frantic grab for them, one of the checks disappears.

"Excuse me. But one of the checks just slipped through the belt," I say.

"You put them on the *conveyor* belt?" the cashier says as she grabs at the rest of the checks.

"Well, yes. I wanted to make sure you saw them."

"You're not supposed to do that." May-I-help-you-Sandy is incredulous at my stupidity.

"Sorry."

"And you're supposed to separate your food according to the items on the check," she says as she roughly reorganizes my order according to the list on the check.

"I didn't know. This is my first time."

She shakes her limp, shoulder-length hair at me as she angrily shuffles the items. A man behind me sighs impatiently. He's in his fifties, handsome, with light-brown hair perfectly streaked with white as though it is purposefully highlighted to look that way. He's wearing a navy Izod golf shirt, tan chinos, and penny loafers (without socks). His grocery basket contains brie, water crackers, red grapes, romaine, and Perrier. *Oh, please.*

"I'd be glad to let you go ahead of me, but she's already started," I say, looking at him apologetically while simultaneously hating that I kowtow to his expensive tastes and important life.

Mr. I-work-out-an-hour-a-day-and-love-to-eat-stuffed-grape-leaves completely ignores me, turns to the woman behind him, and whispers. I bet it's something along the lines of, "Our tax dollars at work." The two of them raise their eyebrows and smile sardonically at one another. She is a stunning woman, also in her fifties, with shocking white, shoulder-length hair. With one hand she positions her tortoise-shelled glasses on top of her head, and with the other she repositions the silk scarf stylishly draped over her shoulder. I feel her eyes look me up and down and realize that whatever she thinks of my body type, clothing, and shoes clearly matches up with her opinion of me for letting my WIC check fall through the conveyor belt's narrow slot.

The cashier breaks through my thoughts. "You can't get these items if the check is gone," she says.

I stand taller. "Well, what happened to the check?"

"It's *under* the conveyor belt!" she says, clearly annoyed. "The people who fix these things will have to get it out the next time they take it apart."

"Fine. I'll just get the rest of the items then."

Sandy sets aside two gallons of milk, and I estimate I'm already out six bucks. Thankfully, another check will give me a free gallon, along with two blocks of cheese. I feel Mr. Perrier shift his weight behind me. He's looking for another checkout line that doesn't have me in it. But checkout lines fill fast in big cities, and there's no guarantee his wait will be lessened if he moves. He puts his basket on the ground and folds his arms across his chest.

"Again, sorry," I say.

He shrugs in response.

"I got WIC!" Sandy suddenly yells.

I jump at her exclamation. "Jeez, you scared me."

Sandy glares at me, along with the dozen or so people from nearby checkout lanes. Everyone wants to see the pregnant lady who has the audacity to obtain free food from this fine establishment. I feel as ashamed as the Fonz at a convent. I'm tempted to grab Stephen's hand, run from the store, and never return, but we're out of milk and almost out of diapers. It's clear that public humiliation is the price I must pay for the fact that Brad and I make very little money.

"I got WIC!" Sandy yells again across the front lines. A short, stocky store manager leaves his Lotto station and punches a few numbers into Sandy's register. I pay for the diapers, put Stephen into his stroller, and stash the free food in the stroller's basket. Shaken, we walk toward home.

Over time, I learn which stores are WIC-friendly and which ones to avoid. I keep a mental list of cashiers who don't scream, "I got WIC!" when they see me in line. I find my chutzpah and debate cashiers who tell me I can't have *crunchy* peanut butter. I laugh when cashiers tell me I can't purchase bags of shredded cheese that are labeled "fancy." (Brie or camembert might be fancy; finely grated cheddar cheese never really qualifies.) And I learn to love the cashiers who try to beat the system by telling me, "Listen, honey. Next time, be sure to come through my line with the jalapeño cheese, and I'll pass it on through." I could care less about jalapeños. It's the cashiers' compassion that makes me want to hug them.

Our second baby, Kristina Marie, is born in the same hospital where, a year earlier, I had surgery to remove an ectopic pregnancy. Kristina is pudgy and beautiful with a head of thick, brown curls. Everything about her is gorgeous. I look into her deep-set blue eyes, and I vow to protect her with the ferocity of a lioness. Under my watch, no one will hurt my baby girl.

When Kristina is a year old, I become an adjunct professor at Eastern College, located outside Philly. I love the job, but adjunct pay is horrible. Still, it helps. It gives us a little much-needed cash and helps me remember that I have a brain. Even with the added income, we still easily qualify for WIC.

Every few months, our WIC certification expires, and I'm faced with a dilemma. I can take my children to their pediatrician and pay a twenty-dollar co-pay to have their fingers pricked and hemoglobin levels checked by professionally trained nurses and doctors. Or I can take my children to the WIC office to have their fingers pricked for free by an untrained clerk. I don't have the extra twenty bucks, so I tell myself everything will be all right if I take them to the WIC office. After all, it's just a pin prick.

Before my WIC appointment, I peel off my teaching outfit (lined skirt, patterned blouse, pantyhose, and sensible navy shoes) and replace it with my WIC-office outfit (T-shirt, jean shorts, and sandals). I put Stephen and Kristina in the stroller and begin my eight-block hike to South Philly. We've been doing the WIC thing for over a year now. It's helped tremendously, but this part never seems to get any easier. I must make a meal of my pride every single time I head to the WIC office or the grocery store.

On my way, I pass a group of young men smoking marijuana, a building where the mafia holds its secret meetings, and an automotive garage where a guy says, "Hey, baby. You lookin' fine!" This in spite of the fact that my hair is yanked into an uneven ponytail, there's a wedding ring on my finger, and I'm pushing my husband's children in a double stroller.

I know I'm getting closer to the WIC office when I'm surrounded by abandoned buildings. I must stroll around shattered glass on the sidewalk to get to the office door, which is propped open. I fold up the stroller and encourage Stephen, now three and a half, to walk up the fifteen narrow steps to the waiting room. If I leave the stroller at the bottom of the steps, it will be stolen. In one arm, I'm carrying one-year-old Kristina. In the other, I'm carrying a thirty-pound double stroller. I am strong and determined. One step after another, with Stephen complaining the entire time, we climb.

Apparently our appointment is scheduled in the middle of employee lunches, so we wait for two long, hot, windowless hours. I can't help but think about my students. What would they say if they could see me now? A few hours ago, I lectured about the looking-glass self to my interpersonal communication class. My students pay big money to learn from me. How might my credibility be trashed if they were to walk into this waiting place and find me with my hair in a ponytail and my shirt stained with breast milk? *What an imposter you are, Eileen. What a fraud.*

After the two-hour wait, I am finally called into the office. It's well over a hundred degrees in here, and beads of sweat make their way down my back. A fan is propped up in the window, but it's as useful as a pinwheel inside a sauna. As the clerk glances through my paperwork, I try to imagine her life. I want to tell her there is more out there than this hellhole. That even if she has a difficult personal life, she could go to school and get an education. I want to tell her she doesn't have to work in this furnace surrounded by tired moms and cranky kids and perfumed with diaper exhaust. But then again, who am I kidding? She probably wants to say the same thing to me.

We're all thirsty and tired. Kristina is still nursing, but Stephen finished his bag of Goldfish crackers an hour ago and is ready to have an all-out meltdown if he doesn't eat something soon. The clerk, whose name is Wanda, reviews my paperwork.

"It says here you're an adjunct professor?" she says.

"That's right."

She looks up at me and squishes up her face. "And you only make three thousand dollars a year?"

"Well, I can only teach one class a semester right now because of the kids and my husband's work schedule."

"Humph. I woulda thought you'd be making a little more money than that!"

"I know. Right?" I say, smiling slightly.

She sighs. "I guess education ain't all it's cracked up to be."

"No. I mean, I love my job and everything, but . . . well, when you look at the money, I guess not."

She changes the subject. "Well, you know we have to check hemoglobin levels today."

"Yeah," I say. "I know."

She moves to the front of her desk with her needles. "Give me your finger," she says to Stephen. Stephen looks at me, his face full of questions. "It's okay, buddy," I say, reaching for his right hand and offering his finger to the clerk.

"It's just a prick," she says as she pokes him. He howls; tears stream down his face as she wraps a plain bandage strip around his finger. There are no Elmo Band-Aids for WIC recipients.

"I'm sorry, buddy. It's okay," I say as he clings to me. My blood pressure, I'm sure, is going through the roof, and I can hardly breathe. *Oh, God. What am I doing here?*

"Next," she says, reaching for Kristina's pudgy little hand. She pokes it, and Kristina screams out, too, crocodile tears streaming down her pudgy red face. But the clerk is obviously new at this, and she fails to draw blood. "I'm going to have to do this again," she says. She swipes Kristina's finger again with the pin, this time cutting more of a gash than necessary.

I compress my reflex to shove the clerk over her own desk as I feel the anger and grief well up within me. In this moment, I swear to myself that this will *never* happen again. All the free milk, cheese, and Cheerios in the world are not worth watching an unskilled clerk take a swipe at my children's fingers with a sharp object. *What am I thinking? Have I lost my mind?*

"Sorry about that," she says, handing me a bandage.

"Um-hm," I say, wrapping the bandage around Kristina's finger while kissing her wet cheeks. Silently, I blink away tears of frustration as Wanda completes the recertification process. With checks in hand, I resolve that something has to change.

Although my experiences in this waiting place are not always positive, most of the time I'm grateful. Being on WIC messes with my politics and taints my black-and-white beliefs with shades of gray. In the future, when I hear others make sweeping generalizations about people in lower socioeconomic groups, my defenses will rise within me. Sometimes I will have to hold my tongue. Other times, I'll let 'er rip.

Sure, there may be some who scam the system, but there are also people like Brad and me who just can't make life add up—despite good educations, careful budgeting, and long hours of hard work. We're here because we've chosen occupations that reward us in ways other than healthy paychecks. We endure these challenges because we love our work and feel as though God himself has called us to do it.

So month after month, we juggle the numbers, tighten our belts, endure visits to the WIC office, and humbly accept our free food. And we wait, sometimes sweat-soaked and frazzled, sometimes frustrated and humiliated, for whatever God has in mind for us when this waiting place is merely a memory that we'll refuse to forget.

9

—⁓—

BREATHE

I am waiting for my baby to cry.

I'm on my hands and knees, scrubbing the floor of the farmhouse we are renting in Fredonia, New York. Since I'm eight months pregnant, my stomach bulges south, and my billowing maternity top sweeps the linoleum. I am not comfortable, but I absolutely must clean this floor. I'm nesting, of course. I've given birth to two babies already; I know how this goes. Memory tells me I attacked the gunk behind the fridge prior to each birth. But this baby is not due for another month, so it must be that I just really, really need to have this floor clean. Now.

Stephen is in school. Kristina is in preschool. And *this* is how

---

I spend my time alone. My mind wanders as I scrub. I think about how much nicer it is to live in this wonderful university town instead of bustling, crowded Philadelphia, where every day in the city felt like a struggle. I thank God for Brad's new job as associate pastor in a place where we can finally afford to live in a roomy house instead of a cramped apartment. The extra space gives us room to think, move, and breathe. Consequently, we are better parents, lovers, and friends. We laugh more now, and the levity is a welcome gift.

As I scrub the crevices, I also think about our family of four, how it will soon become five. Brad and I had many conversations about having a third child. This time, we think we know exactly what we are getting into: another few years of feeding, burping, diapering, crying, and sleepless nights. We don't really *need* another child, but our family, with one son and one daughter, feels a little too perfect to me. Almost a year ago, I told Brad, "I'm ready for a little chaos."

"Chaos?" he said. "Uh, Eileen. I think our lives are chaotic enough."

He was right. After all, he works long hours, including nights and weekends. My job as an adjunct professor at the local university demands additional flexibility on both our parts. And even though we make ten thousand dollars more than we did in Philadelphia, we still qualify for WIC checks. We're hardly raking it in.

Still, we agreed to have one more child. "Who knows how he or she might change the world?" I optimistically told Brad.

"Uh-huh," Brad said, raising his eyebrows skeptically. But I can be very persuasive. Finally, he surrendered, and we headed upstairs to make a baby. (Well, I *suppose* it wasn't quite as simple as that, but with all the things that seem to be so gosh-darn hard, wouldn't it be nice if it were?)

—⁓—

I give birth to a beautiful baby boy. The nurses place him in a nearby bassinet to examine him and suction him out. Although he's covered in blood and fluid, I can see that a large birthmark covers his left arm, from his chest and shoulder to the tips of his fingers. Protective Mama Bear makes an appearance when I look at Brad and say, "When we call everyone to tell them he's here, we're not going to mention the birthmark."

"I know," he says, steadily looking into my eyes.

"I don't want him to be defined by it."

"Right."

"Okay," I say, looking over at Jordan as he lets out his raspy newborn cry. I try to keep the disappointment from showing on my face.

One of the nurses calls our pediatrician to evaluate Jordan before I can hold him. I suspect extra precaution is being taken because of his arm. It's very red, but his fingers are all there, and I breathe a prayer of thanks. Dr. Parikh appears almost immediately, and I know we're in good hands. He's a fantastic doctor, thorough and gentle, with a delightful Indian accent. Brad and I watch as he hovers over our baby and whispers to the nurses. They seem to be taking an extra-long time, but I've never given birth in this particular hospital. Perhaps the extra precaution is protocol.

Dr. Parikh walks to my bedside and gently says in his sing-song voice, "There are some problems with your baby. We need to transport him to Children's Hospital in Buffalo right away."

"Oh," I say, waiting for what comes next.

"We are unable to suction his esophagus. We suspect it is not connected to his stomach."

I stare at Dr. Parikh, noting that his glasses are too large for his small face. He looks back at me, seriously and kindly, gauging my face for glimpses of understanding. I'm trying to absorb this information, but I'm a small sponge being blasted with a fire hose. I don't know how to take it in.

I rifle through my mind to find an appropriate response. My thoughts drift toward the magazine articles I've read about how, even before the umbilical cord is cut, a newborn can instinctively find his mother's breast and begin nursing after birth. I'm fascinated by this concept although I've never been gutsy enough to try it myself. Childbirth is such an extreme sport that I follow whatever rules the medical staff sets for me. Women who prefer home birth freak me out. In my world, "natural childbirth" is an oxymoron. Still, in spite of Dr. Parikh's words, I'm sure I still need to nurse my baby. Certainly, they're not going to take him away before he's had a chance to eat.

"Can I feed him first?" I ask.

"No," Dr. Parikh says, levelly. "If you try to feed your baby, he will drown."

—⚉—

Jordan's primary condition is called EA/TEF (esophageal atresia/ tracheoesophageal fistula), an ostentatious name that means his

upper and lower esophagus failed to connect. His upper esophagus ends at a pouch in the back of his throat. The lower section
is attached to his trachea. His internal plumbing needs rerouting;
immediate surgery is required. An ambulance transports Jordan
to Children's Hospital, located an hour away. I spend the night in
the maternity room, recovering from childbirth. There is no crying
baby in the room with me, no portable crib by my side. Brad goes
home to be with Stephen and Kristina, which is the right thing to
do. I think we both want to pretend that everything is normal. If
we act like everything is normal, perhaps it will be true.

Alone, I try to assess how I feel. It's a little like the time I had
an ectopic pregnancy in that, once again, I'm in the maternity ward
without a baby by my side. I tell myself to breathe in and out. I try
to sleep in spite of the quiet that beats maddeningly in my ears.

—⁂—

Brad and I arrive at Children's Hospital in Buffalo in the early
morning, anxious and tense. I am still quite sore from giving birth
less than twenty-four hours earlier. Before we are allowed to see our
son, we are given an extensive lesson in hand washing: *Use this dis-
posable scrubber brush. Scrub up to your elbows. Brush between fingers
and under nails. Wash for three straight minutes. Here's the clock; be
sure to time it.* As I sanitize my hands, my heart beats wildly inside
me. I want to see my baby. I only held him for a few moments
before he was whisked away. I haven't had the chance to memorize
the curve of his face or the sound of his cry.

Jordan's nurse, Alana, greets us in the hallway and updates

us. He is stable, ready for surgery, and sleeping comfortably. He's been cleared by the surgeon and anesthesiologist. Alana turns to us before entering the neonatal intensive care unit, where at least two dozen infants fight for their lives. "Please don't look at the other babies or ask about them," she says. "It's a privacy issue."

"Okay," I say, fearful at what Brad and I are about to see. We lower our heads and follow her through the maze of incubators and NASA-looking machinery. Out of the corner of my eye, I see babies who are the length and weight of a book. I've seen preemies in magazines and on television. Being in their actual presence is astonishing.

It sounds like a carnival in here, what with all the bells and whistles, chimes, and oxygen pumps keeping time with the babies' vitals. The sound that is alarmingly absent is that of a newborn's cry; every baby is silenced through intubation or drugs. Many have underdeveloped lungs and couldn't cry if they wanted to. We are in a holy Twilight Zone.

Tears spring up in my eyes when I see Jordan, who, at seven pounds, is by far the largest baby in the room. His body almost fills his Plexiglas bassinet. "Hi, Jordan," I say, stroking his fuzzy little head and kissing him repeatedly. I inhale his scent and press it into my soul. Heavily medicated, kept alive by a heartbreaking array of tubes, wires, and IVs, he sleeps on his back without stirring.

"Hey, buddy," Brad says, leaning over him.

I stroke Jordan's cheek with the back of my fingers. "Everything's going to be all right. Pretty soon, you'll come home," I whisper.

Brad and I look at each other with tear-filled eyes. "You know what this means, don't you?" I say.

"What?" he says, bracing himself.

"You're going to have to get him a puppy."

The surgeons meet with us in a small, undecorated room filled with four mismatched hardback chairs and a desk. This is the unadorned space where parents are fed news they should never have to swallow. The surgeons are surprisingly young. I find it both encouraging, because they're fresh out of medical school, and terrifying because they may lack experience. As they explain what they know of Jordan's medical condition, one drinks a Dr. Pepper; the other, an A&W root beer. I realize that one of the most terrifying days of our lives is just another day at the office for them.

I try to digest words like *incision, risks, tracheomalasia, swallow studies, complications, dilatations,* and *reflux.* They tell me that, in addition to his other issues, Jordan has suffered a brain hemorrhage. I then watch as the lead surgeon sketches out Jordan's disconnected esophagus and affected trachea. I try to focus, but my medical learning curve has become a straight vertical line in the last twenty-four hours, and my brain is full of words I can't define. Plus, I'm distracted by the fact that both doctors' eyeglasses are smudged and severely outdated. *How on earth do they see through those things? Don't they make enough money to buy new glasses? Perhaps they don't have time. I bet they work eighty hours a week. Will they be alert enough to save Jordan's life?*

"Do you have any questions?" the lead surgeon asks.

Brad and I look at each other and then to him. I want to say,

Yes, I'd like to know if my son is going to live. I'd also like to know the number of times you've performed this surgery, along with the success and failure rates. Finally, I'd like to know why a handsome, young doctor like yourself is running around with eyeglasses that are two decades old!

"Well. This is a lot to take in, but you did a great job explaining this to us. This diagram," I say, pointing to the sketch that looks like something I might find under my kitchen sink, "is very helpful. So, for now, I think we understand."

"Okay then," the lead surgeon says as he takes a swig of his Dr. Pepper. "Let us know if you have any questions. Now, if you'll excuse us, we need to prep for another surgery."

They shake our hands. We watch them casually walk toward the elevators. Then we walk back to sit with our baby. Back to the waiting place. Only God knows the landscape of the road ahead.

—⬩—

Jordan's surgery is successful, and Brad and I are once again by his side. The tube that runs from his open mouth is taped to his soft, newborn cheeks. I try not to focus on the fact that my baby has become a human pincushion. I count the number of tubes, finding twelve in all. Twelve tubes poking his velvety skin, tiny veins, stomach, penis, and side (to drain his collapsed lungs). Twelve tubes helping him breathe, urinate, and eat. I don't know how to cope with this reality.

All I know to do is pray. But it's difficult to find the words.

I always thought that, if faced with times like these, I would instantaneously become a black belt prayer warrior. I would be on my knees saying all the right words to bring healing to the situation. But tonight I have no words. Every prayer sounds like, *Oh, Lord. Sweet Jesus. Please heal my baby.* So I depend on others to pray for us.

Over the next weeks, whenever I'm not teaching, sleeping, or attempting to be Mom to two other children who need me, I'm at the hospital touching, talking to, or singing to Jordan. When I can find the words, I jot down what I can. Although I desperately want to wake up from this nightmare, I also don't want to forget it. To help make sense of the craziness and desperation I feel, I write:

> *To accept what is,*
> *that is the challenge.*
> *Not to think of what could be*
> *or what caused this.*
> *Not to blame myself. Or God.*
> *But to live in the present moment,*
> *regardless of what it looks like.*
> *To appreciate what I can do:*
> *Touch him,*
> *Sing to him,*
> *Love him.*
> *And not lament what I cannot do:*
> *Hold him,*
> *Feed him,*
> *Fix him,*

Take him home . . . At least not yet.
Life is defined by our ability to hope
and give our feeble, fearful selves over to God.
I vow to trust him and accept what is.
And ask him to hold my little baby in his strong arms,
since I cannot.

We have good days and days I'd sooner forget. One day, I pass a priest as I enter the NICU. "Good morning, Father," I say as I swiftly head over to take my place by Jordan's side.

Everyone in the NICU knows why the priest is here. There is a small room off the entrance to the NICU where families are given complete privacy when a baby is dying. I hear the wheels of the bassinet move across the floor, along with the muffled sobs of the family that packs into the tiny room. The door shuts, and I can hear the hum of the priest's words as he recites last rites to a baby who never had the chance to see sunshine.

I sing to Jordan to keep myself from eavesdropping, but it doesn't help because the room echoes with the baby's final moments. I wonder about the parents and think of how utterly robbed and helpless they must feel. I want to wrap my arms around the mom and let her sob on my shoulder, but I can't because she knows that *my* baby is still breathing.

—⁓—

Weeks pass. Jordan grows stronger. Over time, tubes, stitches, and IVs are removed, and we are able to hold him. I still haven't heard his cry, because whenever he wants to cry, he stops breathing. We know this is bad, so we resolve to do whatever we can to keep Jordan calm, but keeping a baby content at all times is a lot like trying to prevent the tide from coming in.

Doctors are pleased with Jordan's progress and want to release him, but they're puzzled by his "breath-holding spells." The ENT refers to them as "dying spells."

The discharge doctor brings us into his office and tells us to have a seat. "Listen," he says, folding his hands in front of him and leaning across the desk toward us, "I don't like these breath-holding spells your son seems to be having. I want him to go home, but I'm requiring that he be attached to a monitor at all times."

"Sounds good," I say. Jordan seems so fragile. I'm relieved to have something more to depend on than my weary motherly instincts. "Do you think he'll be all right?"

The doctor shifts uneasily in his chair and sighs. "I'm going to be honest with you and tell you that I just don't know. Your baby's not easy to figure out. He has so many unrelated conditions. Usually I can look at a case and say, 'Okay, this plus this plus this equals cerebral palsy,' or, 'This plus this plus this equals Down syndrome.' Jordan is what we call a 'train wreck.' With him, I think, 'This plus this plus this equals *I have no clue*,'" he says, emphasizing his final words.

I nod with understanding, trying not to let my face show the sheer terror I feel. I want to hear the truth. I want the doctor to believe I can handle it. "So, what do we do from here?" I ask.

"You take him home and stimulate him like crazy," he says. "That's what you do."

—∿—

We walk out of the hospital with Jordan, his monitor, multiple pre-scriptions, and referrals for thirteen specialists that Jordan must see, including an ENT, brain surgeon, neurologist, geneticist, and vascular surgeon. As Brad drives home, it feels like we are transport-ing an expensive, invaluable vase that belongs in a high-security museum, not the backseat of our aging Honda.

When one of the monitor's wires comes loose ten minutes into the ride, warning alarms shriek out. I scramble into the backseat to look at Jordan's face. *Are his lips blue? Is he dusky?*

I decide that, for now, he's fine. I wiggle the wires and reattach the leads on his chest and try to regain my composure.

As we head toward home, I wish for a glimpse of the future. If only I knew that everything would be okay—if only God would give me a vision of Jordan as a mischievous three-year-old or a play-ful five-year-old—I'd be so grateful. That reassurance would give me courage to face whatever trials lie ahead. But that's not what happens.

This is one of those waiting places where the only thing you can do is drop anchor, hold one another tightly, and pray for the storm to pass. That's what we do.

10

---〰〰---

CROSSING THE JORDAN

I am waiting for a miracle.

When the waiting place is defined by crisis, there is a lot to learn about family, friendship, and faith. Whenever the cushy layers are peeled away and the nerves are exposed, there is a lot to learn about the stuff we are made of, too.

When Jordan comes home, my dad, who is retired, moves in to help us manage our tricky everyday lives. He's fabulous with Jordan, and he never seems to get weary of having the baby sleep on his round stomach while he watches television. Since Jordan stops breathing whenever we try to lay him down, we all take turns sleeping and holding him. It's insane, but I am willing to carry

---

him upright until he is a senior citizen if it keeps him alive. Dad knows I am "sleeping" upright in a chair every night, so during the day, when I'm not working or trekking Jordan to doctors' appointments, Dad begs me to sleep.

I'm in tune with my baby's every wiggle and need. Even while napping on the second floor of our home, I'm somehow mysteriously connected to him. Although I can't explain it, I know intuitively when Jordan stops breathing. On a few occasions, I startle out of my nap, fly downstairs, and grab Jordan out of Dad's arms just as the alarms begin to sound. I turn Jordan toward me and blow into his face, which shocks him enough to gasp and begin breathing again.

"He was just fine," my dad says, incredulous.

"I know."

"But you were sleeping. How did you . . . ?"

"I have no idea, Dad. I just knew."

Jordan's episodes become more frequent. Recovery from each breath-holding spell becomes more difficult. When the hospital staff trained us to use the monitor, they said that downloading and analyzing the information would be an expensive process; it should only be done, they said, if Jordan's breath-holding episodes warranted our deepest concern. After three weeks of what feels like constant bells and alarms and absurdly blowing into our baby's face, we insist that the monitor be downloaded.

In the late afternoon, our pediatrician calls us with the results. "This is bad. This is very bad," Dr. Parikh says in his accented voice. The monitor documented many legitimate episodes over the past three weeks. On several occasions, Jordan's heartbeat had slowed to a dangerous twenty-three beats a minute. It's possible that he's been deprived of oxygen. Dr. Parikh cannot rule out brain damage. "You need to get him to the hospital right away," he says.

As I listen, relief mingles with terror. We're not crazy after all. It's not really normal to sleep upright in a chair. It's not okay to blow into your baby's face to get him breathing again several times a day. Babies aren't supposed to have dying spells.

By the time we arrive at the hospital the next morning, we are surviving on adrenaline alone. It's been a long, sleepless night filled with dying spells, alarms, and urgent prayers. Doctors take Jordan into surgery to scope his airway and explore the problem. By the time he is in the recovery room, I barely recognize my ashen, weakened infant.

They settle us into the pediatric intensive care unit, where Jordan is hooked up to a new kind of space station. (He's no longer allowed in the NICU. Since he's been in public, he's considered a "dirty baby.") As night falls, Brad leaves the hospital to be with Stephen and Kristina and give Dad a break. Uncomfortably, I settle into a wooden rocking chair and attempt to nurse Jordan. Alarms sound as he stops breathing and turns blue. The medical staff descends on us, grabs Jordan from me, and resuscitates him. They get him breathing, and when they believe he's stable, they leave me with him again. Within fifteen minutes, Jordan is blue, and the whole terrifying ordeal unfolds once more.

If I continue to stay, the medical staff will leave after every episode, and Jordan will continue to have dying spells. But if I walk away, the doctors and nurses will be forced to work on him continually. Perhaps in the process, they'll figure out what's happening. Perhaps they'll keep him alive.

———

So I do the thing I thought I would never do: I leave my baby.

Alarms sound out, and the medical staff descends on us for a third time. With a black airbag, they get Jordan breathing again. They step back and look at me. With tears streaming down my face, I say, "Something's wrong. Something's *really* wrong."

"Yes. We're trying to figure it out, but I gotta tell you, we're just not sure yet," a young doctor says. I'm grateful for his honesty, although I look into his face and see fear. His eyes tell me I need to hope for the best and prepare for the worst.

I swallow and take in a sharp breath. "Listen. I've been awake for the last thirty hours. I can't fight this battle anymore. I need you to do it. I'm going to lie down for a while in that room right there," I say, pointing to the parent room across the ICU. "If you need me, or if something happens, you can get me. But for now, I need to get out of the way so you can figure this out."

"I think that's wise," the doctor says reassuringly. "Don't worry. If anything happens, we'll get you."

I kiss Jordan good-bye, hoping it's not for the last time. I slip into the wallpapered room, shut the door, and sit on a mauve-colored vinyl couch. I pray, *Dear Lord. I can't do this anymore. I thought I could, but I'm exhausted, and I've got nothing left. I give it to you, Jesus. Jordan is yours. I want you to know that, whatever happens next—whether Jordan lives or dies—I trust you, Lord. I trust you.*

The peace that fills the room and covers me is astonishing, as though God himself has pulled me into his lap. The fog of fear lifts, and I can see clearly for the first time in weeks. I lie down on the stiff vinyl couch and curl into a ball to sleep. I have neither a pillow nor a blanket. All I have is trust.

Brad arrives the next morning, and I intercept him before we see Jordan. We sit and talk in the parent room. With an almost-clear mind, I share last night's trauma and holiness. He tells me he experienced a similar turning point during today's drive to the hospital. Like me, he felt God's presence and decided it was time to trust him, regardless of the result. We sit, looking silently into each other's eyes, stunned that God has seemingly met us both in the last few hours. We don't know what's ahead, but we're as ready for it as we ever can be. Together, right there in the parent room, Brad and I dedicate our third child to God.

—w—

Over the next several days, the doctors stabilize Jordan. On Sunday, I attend church for the first time in six weeks. It seems like the right thing to do, given the circumstances. In the lobby, women hug me sympathetically but not pitifully. They tell me they're praying for me and that they're bringing over meals. They offer to watch Stephen and Kristina to give my dad a break. They offer to listen.

One friend says, "I bet you can't believe what you were concerned about a few weeks ago."

"Ha! No kidding," I say. A few weeks ago, I was worried about the price of chicken breasts and whether we'd have enough money for Christmas gifts. Today, the world is a much different place.

Unfortunately, Jordan's complications don't mesh with some of my friends' theologies, so they try to make sense of our situation. Kim, an acquaintance, believes that Jordan's problems are God's way of punishing Brad and me for some latent sin in our lives. (I immediately put Kim on my personal Do Not Call list.) Others want to ask why. But I don't want to talk about why. Babies are born with birth defects. We live in an imperfect, broken world. No child deserves a birth defect, and no mother deserves to watch her child go through hell. This is just the way it is for us. For now.

Inside the sanctuary the congregation worships through song. I stand and close my eyes so I can focus on God and not on the people looking at me sympathetically. Almost instantly, I'm transported to another realm. I am in the ICU and can see Jordan sleeping peacefully on his side with his head tilted up and mouth sweetly open. Standing beside him is Jesus—not the traditional robed-and-sandaled version, but I'm certain it's him nonetheless. He has his hand on Jordan's head, stroking his forehead lightly. Jesus glances over to the main desk, where two nurses sit talking, and then looks back to Jordan. It's such a powerful vision that I continue standing with my eyes closed, tears streaming down my face, long after the song has ended.

Later, I have a renewed sense of hope as I stride toward the ICU for today's visit. I walk off the elevator, pass the waiting room, and open the ICU doors. Then it hits me: I'm one of the fortunate few. Not all are welcome inside a pediatric intensive care unit. In fact, most people wouldn't wish it on their greatest enemies. But I'm blessed to be able to walk through these doors, knowing I belong. Miracles happen here. I know for a fact that God strolls these halls. Courageous battles are fought here. Sometimes the battle is won, and sometimes it's lost, but God is still God regardless. That I know for sure.

As I reach the main desk en route to Jordan's bassinet, I hear a baby crying. "Is there another baby in here?" I ask a nurse.

"Another baby?"

"I hear a baby crying. Is there another baby in here?"

"No," she says. "That's Jordan."

I rush to Jordan's side and find him crying like a "normal" baby. His lips are not dusky or blue. He's not struggling to breathe. His alarms are not sounding out throughout the unit. He's just . . . crying.

"Look at you! You're crying!" I say, pulling him into my arms. "Hey!" I say to the nurses at the station. "He's crying!" I cradle him in my arms as I listen to the most beautiful melody I've ever heard.

—⁂—

This heart-rending waiting place splits my life into *before* and *after*. Before, I was a believer, wife, mom, employee, friend, lover of life. After, I am—and I don't write this flippantly—an eyewitness to a miracle.

The road ahead of us is paved with many hospital visits. We're thankful, heading home, that all of them are round-trips. Jordan will require surgeries, scopes, and swallow studies for his internal issues, in addition to laser treatments for his birthmark. Both a brain surgeon and a neurologist will monitor him closely until his brain bleed fully resolves. He'll require the assistance of thirteen specialists and four therapists. He'll take prescription meds for reflux for the next eight years. But in spite of all that, I'll get the mischievous three-year-old and playful five-year-old I wished for. I will even get a witty, smart, and athletic ten-year-old, which is his age when I finally find the courage to write his story.

Waiting for Jordan to breathe, cry, *live* is a defining waiting place. Over the years, whenever I watch Jordan sleep on his side, I'm transported to the NICU where I see twelve tubes running through his seven-pound body. Whenever he scrapes his knees and runs to me bawling, I stare at his face with raptured curiosity, remembering the times he struggled to breathe. "Life is a breath," the Scriptures say. Living with Jordan reminds me of that.

11

BEHIND CLOSED DOORS

I am waiting for the mail.

I am driving behind a yellow rented Hertz moving truck with tears streaming down my face. *I don't want to move. Oh, I really don't want to move.* Still, here we are, leaving Fredonia, New York—otherwise known as "the town that I love." The people of Fredonia prayed for Jordan, cooked meals for us, baby-sat Stephen and Kristina, and loved us through the most challenging time of our lives. Even so, we are leaving. We are moving to Davison, Michigan, where Brad will become the senior pastor of the Free Methodist Church.

Lord, I don't want to go.

I fix my eyes on the highlighter-yellow truck, an enormous steel box on wheels that holds all our stuff, and follow it west. *It's okay. I've done this before. I can do it again.* But this time feels different. This time, it feels like I'm leaving home.

After four years as an associate pastor, Brad felt ready to lead a congregation of his own. When the call first came to consider moving to Michigan, we immediately refused it. After all, I argued, Jordan was still under the care of several specialists, therapists, and doctors. We had a church and a house, along with friends and neighbors we loved. In addition, I had a great job as an adjunct professor at the State University of New York at Fredonia. Why, I wondered, would we want to give up all that?

A few weeks passed, and my heart softened. We visited Davison. We liked the town and the warmth of the people. We came to realize there were doctors and hospitals and houses and universities in Michigan, too. And we thought maybe—just maybe—God actually wanted Brad to take the job in Michigan. We talked. We prayed. We cried. Finally, we couldn't think of a good enough reason *not* to move to Michigan. ("I don't wanna" doesn't cut the mustard when you're trying to live a faithful life.) Brad and I wrote letters of resignation and said good-bye to coworkers, students, and friends. We sold our house, packed our belongings, hugged neighbors, and backed out of the driveway.

Now here I am, crying all the way to our new house/town/church/life. *Oh, God. Please let this be the right thing.*

This time we are moving into the parsonage right next to the church. We've never lived in a parsonage before, but the idea of a "free house" is appealing, especially when it's as nice as this one.

It's a five-bedroom, two-bathroom house—with a big backyard to boot. Church members have been working hard to prepare the house for us, spending numerous hours cleaning, painting, and fixing. They've installed new flooring and lighting. They've poured love and prayers into us, and they don't even know us yet.

We pull into the church parking lot and are greeted by dozens of church members who are ready to move us into our new lives. I keep my gratitude in check, shake hands, hug, and laugh so I won't burst into tears.

Please, God. Help this to feel like home.

All the boxes are clearly labeled—Kitchen, Living Room, Dining Room, Linen Closet—except for four unmarked boxes that contain all my teaching notes, handouts, and books. "Where do you want these?" Brad asks me. I look from his face to the boxes and back to his face.

"You can put them in the basement."

"You sure?"

"Yep. For now," I say, turning to walk back outside for another armload. *My career is in the basement. How long, Lord? How long?*

—⸙—

Davison is the first place I've ever lived where no one asks me what I do. After living in New York and Philadelphia, where both men and women define themselves by their careers, I should find this refreshing. Unfortunately, I don't. Perhaps it's because I'm often introduced to others with the words, "This is my pastor's wife," as though being the spouse of my husband's occupation is sufficient to define who I am. When I'm introduced as "the pastor's wife," my new acquaintance usually gives me a look-see, inspecting me from head to toe. Frequently he or she says, "You don't *look* like a pastor's wife."

When I'm feeling snarky, I say, "Really? What does a pastor's wife look like?"

I try to adapt, but I keep feeling like I'm on the outside looking in. I know it takes at least six months for a new town to feel like home, so I wait. When six months ends, I switch the benchmark to a year and wait again. Then I give myself an extension to eighteen months. Finally I stop waiting and take matters into my own hands. I decide it's time to get a PhD.

When we moved to Michigan, Brad's parents, Georgia and Winston, moved with us. It was an unbelievable act of courage, love, and generosity. After all, they are in their seventies and have lived in the Southern Tier of New York all their lives. Most people hunker down in their retirement, but Georgia and Winston decided it was time for an adventure.

Georgia is a no-nonsense, down-to-earth woman who supports Brad and me in practical ways. She's ready and willing to watch kids, clean house, and cook dinners while I'm at school if it will help. When she tells Minnie, a fellow parishioner, about my plans to pursue a doctorate, Minnie says, "Why would Eileen want to go and do something like *that*?"

"Because she wants to," Georgia says. "Besides, it'll be good for her. And I think it's great."

This is why I love Georgia. I can trust her with my life.

The closest PhD program is an hour and a half away, but I

don't care. I'm going to lose my mind if the only thing I do is live as a pastor's wife and raise kids in a parsonage. I'm choking to death, and I'm not even wearing a doily collar. I pray, asking God to help me be more supportive of Brad and his all-consuming job. Then I pray some more, asking God to restore my gratitude for the fact that Brad has a job and we have a home. But in the late evening when someone asks Brad to help him with the church's fax machine or when parishioners peek through the front window, catch me napping on the couch, and choose to knock anyway, I run out of prayers. I start to think of ways to leave this waiting place without destroying my family or my husband's career in the process.

—⁓—

I fill out the application and write pithy essays about future goals and past experiences, confident I will be accepted. I graduated with honors from my bachelor's and master's programs. I worked as an adjunct professor at four colleges and have ten years' teaching experience. I have additional experience as a career counselor, a graphic designer, and a corporate trainer. I am absolutely ecstatic. Perhaps this was part of God's plan all along. He not only called Brad to this particular church but also set it up so I can move forward as well. Hallelujah!

The only thing that seems to stand between me and my acceptance is the Graduate Record Examination (GRE). I sign up to take the test and buy study guides and workbooks. It has been ages since I've done algebra and geometry, so I reteach myself the math, loving every moment of it. I haul around hundreds of vocabulary words, memorizing definitions of *recalcitrant*, *misanthrope*, and *fey*. I love words. I love learning. I don't even mind it when someone knocks on my door in the middle of the day, wondering where Brad is since he's not in his office. "I don't know," I say. "Maybe he's going to the bathroom at the church."

"Oh. Well, I thought he might be here," she says.

"Nope. But if I see him, I'll send him over," I say, smiling as I close the door. I go back to studying words: *iconoclast . . . peccadillo . . . sedulous.*

I take my words everywhere and study them whenever and wherever possible: while waiting in the carpool loop (*irascible . . . audacious . . . pugilism*), while waiting in doctors' offices (*assuage . . . venerate . . . fawn*), while waiting for my license at the Department of Motor Vehicles (*nefarious . . . saturnine . . . tortuous*).

I drive an hour on a Saturday morning to take my test. The word *artless* shows up in the goofy analogies three times. I don't know *artless*. I know *anomalous*, but the GRE people don't care about *anomalous*. They want to know if I know *artless* because it's a very, very important word that warrants them asking me in three different ways. I want to *artlessly* smack someone. After taking the test, I drive to a nearby shopping center and buy a Starbucks venti Sumatra coffee and a Cold Stone Creamery double-dip waffle cone. I'm in two-fisted glory.

I count the days. Since I have worked at colleges and universities, I know the flow. My mind follows the envelope containing my GRE scores. I imagine it being processed through the university's Graduate Admissions Office, being sent through campus mail to the Communication Department, and being opened by the secretary. I envision the secretary adding the score to my file where my application and glowing recommendations are already organized. I imagine the busy office staff sorting through hopefuls' applications and being delighted that someone with my qualifications is interested in studying at their school. After all, I have done my homework. I am prepared. I wait.

I become obsessive-compulsive about checking and rechecking the mailbox. I begin stalking it at precisely ten o'clock each morning, checking it every fifteen minutes. At one point, my fifteen minutes coincides with the exact moment the letter carrier arrives at my front door. "Ahh!" I scream.

"I didn't mean to scare you," the mailman says.

"Oh, you didn't. It's just . . . I'm waiting for something."

He raises his eyebrows. "Hope you get it. Soon."

"Thanks." I reach for my daily stack of mail. Today's includes a Rite-Aid weekly flyer, the water bill, and a credit card offer that features three crosses and the message "Jesus Loves You" on the card. The credit card company writes, "Express your faith with every purchase!"

There's something deeply wrong with a world in which you can own a credit card with a full-color picture of Christ's object of torture printed on it.

I keep waiting. I answer telephone calls from parishioners who need my husband. I get more stupid stuff in the mail. I tell myself I'm a patient person. I remind myself that colleges are busy places; perhaps they simply have gotten behind. I call on three separate occasions. Each time, in my nicest, most professional voice, I ask about the status of my application.

Impossible. No one wants me to become a tenured professor more than Elvera, who is one of my dearest friends.

I maintain full eye contact, willing myself not to cry, scream, or pound his desk with my fists. "Dr. Berry's recommendation would have been the first in my file, Dr. Snell. In addition, I called this office on three different occasions to confirm that my file was complete. I was assured that it was." My eye contact is perfect. Perhaps a little too perfect. I am piercing his eyes with my own. I am furious to learn that my future has been dismissed so easily.

Dr. Snell gets defensive as he realizes someone dropped the ball. But he is also a busy man. Applicants like me are dispensable. So what if someone overlooked my information? There are twenty more applicants just like me. He shuffles my "incomplete" papers back into the manila folder, places it on the applicant pile, and folds his hands. "Well, I'm sorry about that."

I swallow hard and soften my approach. "Well. That's okay," I lie. "What can I do to fix this situation?"

"Nothing can be done. It's too late!" he says, clearly flustered. "You'll just have to wait until next year. Certainly, you can wait until next year."

In my heart I know I can't wait. I need to do something to get myself out of my humongous funk. I need to use my brain *now*. Every day in my new life feels like I'm riding a bike that has been stripped of its gears. I press on the pedals, and my foot slips and slips and slips. I'm going nowhere fast. I'm praying, but my prayers feel like they have been stamped with Return to Sender. I've reminded God that he says, "All things work together for good to those who love God." Where, I wonder, is the good in this?

But instead of ranting, I say, "Of course, I can wait. But this is quite disappointing."

"Well, we will look for your application for next year's admission." He stands behind his desk and extends his hand. "It was a pleasure to meet you, Ms. Button."

I take his hand in my own. "It was nice to meet you, too, Dr. Snell. Thank you for your time."

My head is foggy with disbelief as I walk back to my car. Suddenly I become convinced that Dr. Elvera Berry's recommendation is, indeed, somewhere on this campus. I merely need to find it. I replay the application requirements in my mind. Two recommendations were sent via e-mail. But Dr. Berry's was sent snail mail. I conclude that her recommendation is most likely sitting in the Graduate Admissions Office. I turn back toward campus, find the correct building, and ride the elevator to the fourth floor.

"Hi," I say to the work-study student who greets me. "I'm here to collect a graduate recommendation for Dr. Snell." I talk to her like I work here. There's no way she'll give me my recommendation if she believes I'm a prospective student.

"Okay."

"I'm looking for Eileen Button's recommendation written by a Dr. Elvera Berry."

She walks over to the beige file cabinets, pulls out the one that houses the *B*s, and lifts out my file. "Here you go," she says, handing me Dr. Berry's recommendation. "Is there anything else I can help you with?"

I swear I hear the song of a thousand angels pierce the academic air.

"No. This is perfect," I say sweetly. "Thanks so much for your help."

My stride gains momentum as I march my fanny back over to the Communication Department. Ooh, I'm so mad I could bite someone. I must look like a speeding taxi because a homeless man moves out of my way. A bus screeches to a halt when it sees that I'm ready to cross the street. I breathe in and out—using my Lamaze techniques—as I attempt to maintain my composure while climbing to the second-floor offices. When I walk into the Communication Department once again, Dr. Snell is standing next to the secretary's desk. They look at me with *uh-oh* faces as I stride in.

"Here is Dr. Elvera Berry's recommendation," I say, extending the envelope. "It was in Graduate Admissions."

"Wha—," Dr. Snell says.

"Recommendations come directly to you if they are sent online. But if they are sent through the mail, they're channeled to Graduate Admissions."

"It doesn't matter," Dr. Snell says. He is embarrassed, but he's also tired of me. "I told you. It's too late!"

"I understand. I simply want to have my file completed in your office."

"You may apply again next year," Dr. Snell says. "I will also give you permission to take a class in the fall. You must pay for it, of course. But you may take it."

"Thank you. I will consider it. I appreciate your time. Have a good day," I say as I exit the office.

I am too angry to cry. Too fired up to sulk. Throughout my life I have been able to wriggle out of the waiting place and escape before it chained me down. I am left without a plan. For now, my career will remain in cardboard boxes in the basement. I am officially stuck waiting for something to happen that I have yet to define. I want—need—something to happen quickly. For sanity's sake, I simply cannot be *just* a mom and a pastor's wife. I don't want to be defined as the spouse of my husband's occupation any more than he wants to be defined as the spouse of *my* occupation. (If I had one, that is.)

Suddenly it feels like I have been waiting a really long time at a bus stop, only to be told that the bus no longer follows this route. I could attempt to find the new route, but now I'm not sure I want to travel where it's headed.

It's time to regroup. Think. Pray. Wish. Dream. I'm convinced I need a new destination and a new path far away from this one. I can't move back home to New York, and I can't move forward. Yet.

They say when God closes a door, he opens a window. I say that when God closes a door, sometimes he slams it in your face.

If only God would give me a peek into the future. Just a peek. Then I would know that soon I will be inspired to write a commentary that will open the door to becoming a newspaper columnist and author. I would know that once again I will be standing in front of a classroom as an adjunct professor, fiercely loving both my students and profession. I would know that there *is* hope and that God wasn't kidding when he promised to work all things together for good.

But all those possibilities are hidden behind closed doors for now. Today I can only hunker down, pray harder, and listen more keenly. I may not know where I'm going, but I will wait for as long as it takes. I will. And I will hold tightly to the belief that something good is yet to come.

12

REDEEMING THE BVM

I am waiting for my father-in-law to dispose of Mother Mary.

The house is perfect. After living two years in the church parsonage, trying to figure out when Brad-the-pastor was working and when Brad-the-husband-and-dad was home, we buy a house a mile away from the church. Since I see myself as an urban, brownstone kinda girl, it's hard to believe that we purchased a house (a *tract house*, no less) in the suburbs. Still, it's the right place for us at this time in our lives.

The small midwestern town of Davison is where we live; we'd best make the most of it. The kids love the fact that the neighborhood is filled with children who are ready to play. I love the retro-feeling kitchen with the big window that looks onto the backyard. The yard is enclosed by a chain-link fence, which all but guarantees us a dog. And let's face it; no childhood is quite complete without the memory of a drooling canine dumping a daily load on the lawn.

There is one thing about the house that is a bit disturbing: it comes with a three-foot, 185-pound concrete statue of the Blessed Virgin Mother. She stands in the overgrown flower bed in the back of the property.

I like Mother Mary. I really do. My Catholic upbringing taught me to revere her, and I know all the words to the rosary. I just never imagined Mary's concrete likeness standing in the middle of my black-eyed susans.

Once we obtain ownership of the house, Brad and I survey the flower-bed mess that extends across the back of the property. It's obvious that the former owners once took great pride in their garden, now overgrown with goldenrod and thistle. In her faded blue robe, Mary stands, head bowed, in the middle of the mess.

I step through the weeds, grab hold of Mary's head, and attempt to jiggle her back and forth. She doesn't budge. "What're you doing?" Brad asks.

"I'm trying to move her. If she's not heavy, I'll pick her up and put her on the curb."

"You're gonna put her on the curb?"

"Yeah. Someone will want her. They'll never see her if she's back here."

"Give me a break, Eileen. No one's gonna want that. Besides, there's no way you can move her. She weighs a ton."

"Then get over here and *help* me," I say.

"Babe. She's too heavy. Forget it."

"What are we gonna do with her then?"

"I dunno," he says, shrugging. He walks away to survey the thistle and goldenrod growing in the side yard instead. I know Brad well enough to understand that he needs time and space to think about this problem. That doesn't mean, however, I won't take matters into my own hands.

It won't be easy. Just yesterday, we sat across from the former owners, Chet and Jouella, at the closing table at the Realtor's office. Jouella was an animated firecracker, but Chet sat quietly in his wheelchair, his body ravaged by the effects of Parkinson's disease. Their move into a retirement community with nursing assistance meant they were giving up their home, their yard, and their independence. I quickly realized that our new home signified a beginning for Brad and me—and an ending for them. While we excitedly waited for the keys to our house, they sadly waited for their lives to end.

With as much sensitivity as possible, I asked Jouella what she would like us to do with the statue of Mother Mary.

"Just put a bag over her head and crack her up," she said matter-of-factly.

I was mortified. While I didn't think she would say, "Oh, honey, just haul her on over to the nursing home," I wasn't prepared to simply "crack her up." After all, Mary's likeness had stood in the garden for a very long time. I was sure that she had been a comfort to them as they aged. I imagined Jouella standing in her kitchen window with a dish towel flung over her shoulder, watching Chet, before he got sick, working in the hot summer sun, meticulously maintaining their lawn. I'm sure she had a certain kind of comfort knowing that Mary's likeness watched over him, too.

No, I would not simply "crack her up." Someone else would have to do it. Someone strong. Someone brave. Someone who couldn't recite the Hail Mary if his life depended on it. I would call upon my father-in-law.

Winston Button is a former dairy farmer who has never been Catholic. He's a master at weed whacking and a pro at lawn maintenance. Since he grew up Baptist, I figure he'll have no emotional connection to Mother Mary—no memory of a priest reciting in a monotone, "Hail Mary, full of grace, the Lord is with thee . . ." as he leads the congregation in reciting the rosary. My father-in-law is the perfect criminal to perform the dirty deed.

When Dad comes over to weed whack the goldenrod, I make my pitch. "Dad, I need you to do me a favor."

"What?" he says with an eager look on his face. I love his wide-eyed expression. He adjusts his hat as if doing so will give him the gumption to take on whatever deed I need him to do.

I take a deep breath and look him in the eye. "I need you to get rid of Mother Mary."

"The statue?"

"Yes."

"Well, I . . . What do you want me to do with her?"

This is going to be easier than I thought. "I don't know. Just break her up, I guess."

"Break her up?" he says.

"Yes! Come on, Dad. It's just a statue." *Chicken.*

"Well, I know that, kid," he says. I love that he calls me "kid" even though I'm in my early forties. One day he will be a hundred years old, and I will be sixty-seven, and I'll still be "kid."

"It's just . . . are you sure?" he asks.

"Yep. Will you do it?"

"I'll take care of it right away," he says, and he walks toward the garage to retrieve our large hammer.

I busy myself in the upstairs while my father-in-law performs the dirty deed. I would help him, but, you know, I'm busy, busy, busy. I fold linens, hang clothes, and clean the bathroom. I make as much noise as I can to keep myself from hearing the metal hammer strike the concrete. I shudder when I think of what my uncle Tom would say if he knew about this. Uncle Tom loves the Blessed Virgin Mother. Although he is my godfather, he missed my wedding because of a pre-planned pilgrimage to Medjugorje, Yugoslavia, where he hoped to glimpse an apparition of the Blessed Virgin Mother. I'm certain he would be horrified that his goddaughter would be willing to crack up her image. Then again, he lives six hours away. I tell myself he'll never know.

As I swish Comet around the toilet bowl, I remind myself that the statue is only a piece of concrete. It's merely symbolic. Still, this would be a lot easier if the mortar had been poured into a different mold other than the one resembling Jesus' mama. If the former owners had left behind a concrete frog or garden gnome, for instance, I'd be able to destroy it myself in a heartbeat.

"Ei-leeeen!" my father-in-law calls from downstairs.

"Yeah?" I holler back.

"Come here!"

I descend the stairs and follow my father-in-law's voice to the backyard. He's only been out there a few minutes. I can't imagine he's finished already. *Dang. Mother Mary must be in pieces in the backyard.* I'm relieved the act is over, but I'm not interested in seeing the carnage.

Dad is on the back patio, waiting for me. He wears a blended expression of mischief and pride. "I've taken care of Mary," he announces.

I immediately detect the lack of guilt in his voice. There's no way he's "taken care of" Mary this fast.

"Where is she?" I ask, looking around. She's nowhere in sight.

"Never mind," he says.

"Dad," I say, looking him square in the face and placing my hands on my hips. "Where is she?"

"Well . . . ," he says, pausing. I know he wants to tell me. He's never been terribly good at keeping a secret. He leans down close to me and whispers the words, "I buried her."

"What?" I say, leaping back. I'm both amused and appalled.

"Sh!" he says. His eyes dart around the yard as if the police or the Catholic Diocese might overhear our conversation. "Now listen. Don't say another word about it."

I lower my voice and whisper, "But I thought you were going to get rid of her."

"I was. But they say it's good luck to have Mother Mary buried in your yard." He states this with great authority and conviction, beckoning me to follow him across the yard. He is as certain of Mother Mary's luck as he is that corn must be "knee high by the Fourth of July" if the crop is to be successful.

———

"I can't believe you buried her," I say.

"Well, it's done," he says, standing by her grave. Dad buried her in the middle of what will one day be my shady flower garden. A piece of her base sticks out of the ground.

"Shouldn't she be buried a little deeper?" I ask, kicking the protruding piece of concrete.

"Trust me, kid. She's fine."

—⁓—

Our family adds a puppy, a yellow labradoodle, to our mix. Sadie Rae is a champion digger. She digs up my tulip bulbs and eats them. She digs up my rose bushes and uses them as chew toys. From my kitchen window, I watch her grab hold of five-year-old Jordan's T-shirt and drag him across the yard.

When Sadie Rae discovers Mother Mary, she's delighted by the challenge, and clumps of dirt go flying. Once she exposes Mary's faded blue robe, I decide to take Mother Mary's disposal into my own hands. After all, I have a vision for my backyard that includes a huge vegetable garden, fruit trees, a clothesline, and wild flowers. There's no room for the Blessed Virgin Mother, especially one sticking halfway out of the ground. While Brad is at work, I decide to move her myself.

I head to the garage, grab the wheelbarrow and a shovel, and steer the tools into the backyard. Carefully, I exhume the Blessed Virgin Mother, finishing the job that Sadie Rae has started. I can't lift the statue, so I shuffle her toward the wheelbarrow. I tilt the wheelbarrow up and lean Mother Mary onto it. When I attempt to right the wheelbarrow, the weight of her body causes it to tip to the left, and Mary thumps into the grass. I lose my balance and land on top of her. If the neighbors are watching, they're getting quite a show.

I finally wrestle her rigid, 185-pound body into the center of the wheelbarrow and begin to push. The front wheel flattens as I steer her toward the front of the house. Miraculously, I get her out of the wheelbarrow and stand her up in the garage. I call the local Catholic church.

―∿―

I know this church fairly well because I regularly slip through its front doors to spend some time praying and thinking in quiet. I know a lot of people who try to shake off their spiritual upbringing in exchange for a new and improved version. I'm not one of them. I may be a Protestant pastor's wife, but my defenses rise within me when I hear people bash Catholics.

Non-Catholics don't understand the beauty, ritual, and heritage. Neither can they understand the holy feeling I get when I swing open the church's heavy wooden doors and breathe in the lingering scent of incense. I dip my fingers into the fount of holy water and make the sign of the cross, touching my forehead, heart, left shoulder and right shoulder as I whisper, "In the name of the Father, Son, and Holy Spirit."

I feel the water dry as I make my way up the aisle to the middle pews, where I genuflect and make the sign of the cross again. Carefully, I pull the knee-rest down and bow to pray as I consider the life-sized crucifix, the image of the Blessed Virgin Mother holding baby Jesus, and the stained-glass windows depicting the stations of the cross. I may not be Catholic anymore, but I love this place. The holy quiet. The familiar smell. The feel of the cushion beneath my knees. Its aching familiarity makes me miss it.

—⁓—

Marilyn, the church's receptionist, is sweet and assures me that someone in the church will be interested in my sacred lawn ornament. I'm relieved until she asks, "Is the statue in good shape?"

"Well," I say, "she's about forty years old." *Uh . . . like me.* "And she's been buried for a few months." *I've spent many months feeling buried, too.* "And . . . well, I'm sure she's not as pretty as she used to be. A lot of her paint is chipped off." *Ditto.*

Marilyn pauses. "O-kaaay," she says. "Well, I'm sure someone will get back to you in the next few days."

What a shock. No one does.

Time marches on. Brad and I update the house, changing light fixtures and flooring. We haul junk out of the basement and place it all in the garage. Mother Mary seems to survey it all. We hire a man to haul our junk away and ask him to take the statue as well. "Listen, I'll take just about anything, but I don't mess with the Blessed Virgin Mother," he says. He piles the junk into the back of his beat-up pickup truck. Mother Mary stands alone in the now-clean garage.

Every time I open the garage to get dog food, I see her. Every time I retrieve the garden shovel to plant a hosta or a carpet rose,

I give her a little smile. I stop thinking of ways for her to disappear and start thinking of ways to keep her. Somewhere in the midst of my comings and goings, I decide to put her back where she belongs—in our garden. I figure it's now my turn to attempt to create something beautiful from the dirt beneath her silent gaze.

I wrestle her back into the wheelbarrow and haul her into the corner of my garden. I build a concrete platform and set her onto it. I brush off the dirt and hose her down. Once she's dry, I hand my twelve-year-old son, Stephen, a can of cream-colored spray paint, and he paints her from head to toe. *There, just like new, except her face is now the same color as her formerly blue robe.*

I'm scattering some rocks at her feet when my neighbor Joyce calls out my name. "Hi, Eileen," she says, walking toward our fence.

Uh-oh. "Hi, Joyce," I say, dropping the last of the rocks and wiping my hands on my shorts.

"I see you've decided to keep the statue," she says, reaching me. It's more of a question than a statement. Joyce attends the Baptist church. She knows I'm a pastor's wife. My decision to keep the Blessed Virgin Mother won't be easy for her to understand.

"Yeah. Stephen painted her. Don't you think she looks better?"

"Uh, yes," she says because she has no idea what to say. "You moved her, too."

"Yep. Thought she worked better over here." The statue is closer to her property now, so I add, "Hope it's okay with you."

"Well . . . ," she says hesitantly. "I *guess* it's all right. As long as you don't pray to her or anything."

"Hey, you never know. I just might." This is the part of my personality that always gets me into trouble. I like to shake things up.

Joyce laughs nervously. "You wouldn't . . ."

"Nah. Don't worry. But I might have to plant some flowers at her feet."

"Oh."

"Yeah. Seems to be the right thing to do."

―∼―

Once in a while, when you stand in the waiting place long enough, you change your mind. I thought I wanted to get rid of a statue, but what I ended up keeping is a holy reminder of my childhood and family history. Had I not been forced to wait, I might have missed out on realizing that. The lenses through which we see the world are always changing.

Almost every day I think about our home's previous owners. Whenever I yank weeds in the summer sun, I think of Chet. I imagine him taking a break from his weeding and looking at the Blessed Virgin Mother's peace-filled face, reminding him that anything of value in life takes determination, faith, and perseverance.

Whenever I wash the dishes or make dinner, I think of Jouella. I imagine her looking out of her kitchen window to see the Blessed Virgin Mother's likeness, reminding Jouella to be loving and patient with her husband and family.

Sometimes all we need is a concrete reminder to recognize we are surrounded by the sacred.

13

SUNDAY, SUNDAY

I am waiting for church to be over.

She is loving and life changing; she is malicious and overbearing. She is beautiful; she is ugly. She is as light as day, capable of astonishing kindness and generosity; she is as dark as night, capable of unspeakable evil. I love her; I hate her.

She is The Church.

She is often referred to as the "bride of Christ," but she can be a mighty horse of a bride. Trust me, I live with her. In Brad's and my life together, she is "the other woman." For almost twenty years, I've observed her up close and personal, and I've seen firsthand that she can be graceful, merciful, and safe. But she also can be demanding, nitpicky, and mean. There are days she's more interested in making sure people behave properly than encouraging them to take leaps of faith. And she gets caught up in hurtful debates about things that don't amount to a pile of hooey.

Although for six days a week Brad tries to balance his time between her and me, Sundays are hers alone. And guess what? Sunday comes. Every. Single. Week. This may not be a huge revelation for the average Josephine, but it's been a surprise to me. In a pastor's home every Sunday is a workday. It doesn't matter if someone else is preaching; there are still announcements to make, an offering to account for, and people who require the personal touch of their senior pastor. On top of it all is the persistent knowledge that the next sermon . . . the next service . . . the next Sunday looms just seven days away.

In a pastor's home, there is no such thing as a "weekend." Saturdays are often spent putting final touches on Sunday's sermon. Even if the sermon is written, it's being mulled over, hogging any available space in a pastor's mind. Although most pastors (including my husband) would say that it's a privilege and a calling to speak God's Word to a congregation, it's not easy to watch Brad wrestle week after week.

—✺—

I am sitting in the front pew listening to my husband preach. I don't enjoy sitting here. People watch me. I know that Brad wants me to sit up front with him because he doesn't like to sit alone. I don't like sitting alone either. I rarely get to listen to the sermon while sitting beside my husband because, most of the time, he's delivering it.

Today, Brad is preaching on the value of silence. "Be still, and know that I am God," he says, quoting the Scriptures. There is a "time to keep silence, and a time to speak."

People nod their heads to show agreement. I can't help but wonder if they realize it's impossible to be silent when cell phones are ringing. Just moments ago, someone's rang, effectively demonstrating that we are forever "on" and accessible in this world. I'm sure the parishioner is embarrassed, but the ringtone provided a timely example for the rest of us to consider.

Brad continues his sermon. He says we find silence uncomfortable, sometimes unbearable. He says that instead of leaning into the silence and listening to what it has to tell us, we tend to decorate it with noise. To drive home the point, he stops speaking and stands silently for a moment, scanning the congregation. Then he steps out from behind the pulpit, descends the stairs, and sits next to me. Quietly, we wait for what will happen next.

Parishioners shift impatiently in their seats. Someone blows his nose. Someone else unwraps a peppermint candy. I sit with my hands folded in my lap and my head slightly bowed. I have an amused look on my face because I can feel the congregation's discomfort. *It's a good thing we're not Quakers*, I think. *We'd never be able to stand the tension.*

A few seconds pass. A child innocently yells out, "Hey! Where'd that guy go?" Someone behind us begins clapping and chanting, "We want more! We want more!" I giggle silently to myself. The crowd can't take the pressure. It's unbelievable, really. *Great illustration, babe.*

After thirty seconds, Brad slowly stands and makes his way back to the pulpit to resume speaking. The congregation breathes a sigh of relief to have its pastor back where he belongs. The seat beside me is empty once again.

As Brad finishes his sermon, I think about the modern-day church. There are days when it feels to me that hundreds of people show up to watch my husband do his job. Why, I wonder, do altars feel like stages and congregations feel like audiences? Isn't there a way we could do this differently?

Brad concludes his message and asks the congregation to stand for the final blessing. "May you experience God's holy silence today and in the days to come. In the name of the Father, Son, and Holy Spirit," he says. I know that behind me in our Protestant congregation a half dozen Catholics are making the sign of the cross on their bodies as he says this. I am always tempted to do the same, but I don't. Brad doesn't need me to freak anyone out.

As I collect my purse from underneath the pew and retrieve my church program, Grace approaches me. I like Grace. She's tall and stately, with eyes so dark they're almost black. "Eileen, Eileen. I need to talk with you about something."

I assume it has something to do with my weekly *Flint Journal* column. Many parishioners read the column faithfully and are proud of the fact that their pastor's wife is regularly published. Since I'm not particularly active in the church's ministries, the column gives the congregation a way to get to know me. They often tell me, "I don't always agree with you, but you always make me think." I couldn't ask for more.

"Hi, Grace. How are you?" I ask.

"Fine. Fine. Listen, I just need to tell you something." She takes a deep breath and plows ahead. "I need you to know that I am very disappointed by how you acted during the sermon."

I feel the color drain from my face. My blood runs cold. *What?*

"When Pastor sat down next to you during the silent moment, you didn't sit quietly with him. You laughed!" she scolds.

"I did not laugh," I say levelly. "My shoulders may have slightly bounced, but that's only because I was responding to the things going on around me."

"But nothing was more important than that moment. Nothing. Your laughter was very distracting."

Is she joking? She doesn't look like she's joking. I try to smile pleasantly, but my expression is tight. In my peripheral vision, I see that people are filing out, heading toward the fellowship hall to eat donuts. They'll chomp up all the apple fritters. Every week, the apple fritters are the first to go.

"Grace, did you hear that child say, 'Hey! Where'd that guy go?'" I ask.

"Yes, I did."

"And did you hear that woman say, 'We want more! We want more!'?"

"Yes."

"I was responding to that. I wasn't laughing at Brad's silence." I remind myself to stay loose and open-minded and not fold my arms across my chest. I might want to crawl into a hole, but I don't want to put up any unnecessary walls.

"Well, it's important for me to tell you that it was a holy moment for me. I sensed the presence of God. And you were a *distraction* to it." She's so upset she's about to cry.

I attempt to find my contrite heart, but I'm pretty sure it's in the fellowship hall eating donuts with everyone else. "I'm sorry I was a distraction, Grace. I'll be more aware of my actions in the future." My words are cold and measured. I cannot find the strength or the will to warm them. I'm mad. Furious, actually. The idea that my blink, expression, and shoulder bounce are being observed and analyzed for their spiritual merit makes me absolutely insane.

I walk through the doors of the sanctuary, suddenly sick to my stomach. I'm feeling defensive, angry, and embarrassed. I may not always love the bride of Christ, but I definitely don't want to be a distraction. I need to get outta here. Now.

I search the lobby for my children, but they're nowhere in sight. My friend Sasha sees me. "Whoa," she says. "You okay?"

"Yeah. It's just . . ." With eyes flashing, I tell her the story.

"Are you serious?"

"Oh, I'm serious. Un-freaking-believable, isn't it?"

"Actually, it's a little funny because Veronica just told me she saw you laugh during the silent time. She said she didn't appreciate it either."

I cannot believe this. "Oh, great. Now the whole stinkin' world is analyzing my nonverbals?"

"I guess so. Lucky you."

—◊◊—

On subsequent Sundays, I settle into the *back* row of the church. This is a much better place for me. I'm not being spiteful or childish; I'm just done being a sanctuary ornament. I need to attend church, too.

The back row is, by far, the best seat in the house. I am surrounded by stragglers, crying babies, and people trying to figure out if they like the church enough to come back. No one recognizes me here. My love and compassion are more accessible to me.

I watch Brad stroll into the sanctuary and take his seat in the front pew. His hair is gray, making him look much older than his early forties. He looks lonely although we both know he's not alone. Until this day is over, the mistress will be whispering in his ear. Today and every Sunday, she has his full attention.

Between Brad and me is a mishmash of humanity. From this vantage point, it's easier to see that I am surrounded by imperfect people just like me. We do our best to live our faith one day at a time. We fail miserably. We get our feelings hurt and hurt one another's feelings. We regularly fall on our faces. Once in a while our faith gives us the strength to scrape ourselves off the pavement. When it doesn't, we hope that someone will soon come along to gently help us to our feet again.

From the back pew I see the lovely (and not so lovely) people who make up The Church.

They are the divorced and dying, grumpy and grateful. They have been blessed beyond measure; they have survived astonishing loss. They have doubted God and chosen to love him in spite of it all. Like me, they often wonder about this peculiar place. Like me, they come here to seek him.

Week after week, they clumsily work out their personal faith. Some shout, "Yes!" or, "Amen!" during the sermon. Others refuse

neighborhood children would come to the door and ask if she can come out to play.

As I watch this little girl and her mother, I can't help but think that they are who this church is for. The church exists for broken people who know that life is too precious and too precarious to dare live it on their own. Brad, referring to a statement by Archbishop William Temple, often says the church is the only organization that exists for the benefit of its nonmembers. He believes it wholeheartedly. The members, however, are not so sure.

Most everyone in the church will tell you that their personal relationship with Jesus is crucial. But there are days when Jesus gets lost in the clutter of our everyday lives and petty concerns. There are days we grumble about worship-song selections. (Some of us like hymns; some of us like to rock.) We complain when someone else sits in "our pew." Our panties get bunched up in a wad when someone on the worship team shows too much cleavage. We know the verse that reads, "The first will be last, and the last first," but we race each other to the front of the potluck line and never notice the irony.

When we're not driving each other crazy, we try to love each other. It's not easy. We gossip and judge and hurt one another. We love and support and pray for one another. There are days our words and actions cut deep enough to draw blood. Sometimes, we say we're sorry. Sometimes, we don't.

The soloist walks to the podium to sing. She's fantastic. She always is. She's talented enough to be on *American Idol*, but she's not interested in fame or fortune. She has a good job, a good husband, and two precious children. Her son has a muscular disorder that threatens his very life. In the face of that reality, she stands and sings of grace and faith and mercy and love. Every time she sings, people weep.

Brad stands and, once again, preaches his guts out. He's a passionate, organized speaker. He's funny and intense. Despite that, at twelve o'clock, people's watches start beeping their noon alarms. Some stop listening. They shuffle restlessly in the pews and get ready to leave even though Brad is still speaking. I want to elbow them and say, "Pay attention! Don't you realize my husband has poured blood, sweat, and tears into this message?"

My frustration is not about them, really. It's about me. I can't help but be jealous of these people who will leave this place and not revisit it for another week. When the service is over, they will head to Tim Horton's, Wendy's, or Old Country Buffet. They might discuss the sermon. They might not. They will get on with their lives, which will (hopefully) include God, but not (necessarily) The Church. There are days when she's such a burden, I wish someone else would take her home for a while. I've asked Brad if he'd like me to schedule him a lobotomy to free him from her. He just smirks or sighs in response.

Brad concludes his sermon with a blessing and then shakes hands in the lobby. He checks to make sure the doors will be locked. Our family climbs into the minivan, and The Mistress hitches a ride home. She nestles herself into Brad's lap so she can whisper painful reminders into his ear. *I can't believe how you misspoke in the middle of the sermon. How embarrassing . . . Can you believe so-and-so came back this week after the hateful e-mail he sent you? I wonder what he's thinking . . . Did you hear that Gene is in the hospital again? You'll be sorry if you don't visit him this afternoon.*

Of course, I can't hear her exact words, but I can see that her silent reminders make Brad wince. I watch as she beats him up from the inside. I try to make conversation. I try to make him laugh. I try to make him forget her for a while, but it's impossible to listen to The Church and to me at the same time.

When we get home, Brad eats lunch with the kids and me. But when the kids ask him questions, he doesn't answer. Instead he looks at us the same way a kid wearing headphones looks at his parents while his music is blaring. No matter how Brad tries, he can't free himself from her barrage. *Where was so-and-so this week? Someone told me she was church-shopping again. I can't believe she would leave so soon after you officiated at her mother's funeral.*

Since The Church is whispering into Brad's ear, distracting him, the kids ask me questions they should be asking him. "Is Daddy coming to my soccer game today?" Jordan asks me.

"I don't know. Why don't you ask him? He's right there!" I say, exasperated, pointing to the head of the table.

"Dad, are you coming to my soccer game today?" Jordan asks.

Brad looks straight ahead as The Church whispers, *Don't forget that the nominating committee is meeting tonight. And remember that you scheduled two meetings on your day off.*

"Dad?" Jordan says. "Dad?"

I always hope a child's voice will break her spell. It rarely does.

—⁂—

Every Sunday I walk through the doors of this waiting place. Sometimes I enter just because I'm supposed to, and I'm stunned that God chooses to meet me here in spite of my poor attitude.

Other times I search for him, but too many other things cloud my vision; I end up seeing only dust. No one ever said that waiting for the holy should be easy.

As for The Church, I like her; I loathe her. She delights me; she disappoints me. I want her; I want to disown her. There are days when I count the minutes until I get to leave. There are days I've run into her arms, weeping. Although I realize how dysfunctional and codependent it sounds, I need her. There are still days when there's no place else I'd rather be.

14

—ᴍᴍ—

STEPPING INTO DARKNESS

I am waiting for my husband to come home.

In the middle of every Sunday service, between the songs and the prayer, the worship leader invites the congregation to bring their cares forward. The altar is quickly lined with people living in the midst of their waiting places. It takes courage to step away from the pew's comfort and walk toward God in front of everyone, but sometimes life beats us up so badly we have no other choice.

This morning, more than a dozen people have stepped to the front, in need of a special touch from God. There's the aging couple dealing with multiple health issues, the young couple working to save their marriage, and the unemployed GM worker hoping next month's mortgage payment will fall from the sky. Kneeling nearby is the divorced woman who struggles with loneliness, the teen who prays for her alcoholic mom, and the woman whose husband was killed when the car he was repairing crushed him. (The woman prays especially for her four-year-old daughter who found him under the car and thought he was just sleeping.) Finally, there's a close-knit family, holding one another. Their son/brother/grandson has been deployed to Iraq. Together they seek God and try to stay strong.

As their pastor, Brad knows each story. He shares in the holy and unholy moments in people's lives. When possible, he does what he can to ease the burdens. Some believe he's been blessed with a direct line to God, so when things don't work out, they wonder if he's praying hard enough. Others would like him to provide easy answers to release them from their waiting places. He'll walk through the deepest waters, but he's merely a man. Since he's a big man, it's often assumed that he can carry a heavy load on his broad shoulders. Because I live with him, I know he's more fragile than he looks.

Taking on the grief and anguish of others can be dangerous. Pain is cumulative, and a minister is limited in what he can handle. Pressed-down pain has the potential to become an emotional time bomb that can explode and lead to great darkness. Brad and I both search for the release valve, but it's not easy to locate through all the layers. I am desperate to relieve him of the burdens that only God is strong enough to handle.

—◊◊◊—

Brad lies flat on our bed and tells me about the pressure in his chest—the weight of ministry threatening his aorta. Literally and figuratively, his heart aches for people. He lies immobilized, his six-foot, six-inch, 275-pound body looking almost frail pressed against the mattress. The load of ministry is heavy, and he has a desire to sleep and keep sleeping—or to run away, perhaps.

But there's no time for that. The sermon is calling. So is the need to identify the next sermon series. He has an appointment to discuss Compassionate Ministries and a meeting with a member who doesn't think the church is doing enough for missions. He needs to follow up with a parishioner who is upset that Brad didn't visit him during his short hospital stay and now is threatening to leave the church. (Unfortunately, Brad was unaware the man was even *in* the hospital.) He also has another funeral to prepare for. The third in two weeks.

No doubt, this particular funeral will be one of the hardest. Brad's friend Mark has lost his wife, Linda.

Here's what I believe: God doesn't always save us from our brokenness. He lets us decide, even with our clouded capacities, what we will do. Sometimes we call on God, and he seems to answer. Sometimes we call on God, and a deafening silence fills the line. Brad says that nothing happens in our lives that does not first pass through the hands of God.

Do I believe this? God is good, but we are a mess when left to our own devices.

I've been attempting to live a faithful life long enough to know that stories don't always end the way they're "supposed" to. I've read many wonderful stories in Christian publications where the format is: (1) I had a problem, (2) the problem was serious, and I hit rock bottom, (3) God did a miraculous thing and saved me, and (4) I am a new creation. Hallelujah! Glory to God!

———

But this neatly tied story is not the only reality we know.

Sometimes the story ends without the hope-filled conclusion. People die. Marriages end. Depression wins. And pastors implode. Sometimes life as we knew it, and had dared to dream it, is destroyed with no second chances. It feels like God looks away, tragedy sneaks in, and we spend the rest of our lives haunted by the ensuing fallout.

There are times when we are left only with what feels like the wrong ending. When we listen closely enough, we think we hear the angels cry.

—⁂—

I drag myself into the church for the funeral, afraid of what I will see. I'm not the only one; everyone else in the parking lot walks toward the building in the same slow motion. No one rushes toward sorrow.

There are funerals that are celebrations of well-lived lives. And then there are funerals that are filled with answerless questions and silent screams. This is one of them.

I enter the lobby and am relieved that mourners are chatting noisily. Perhaps too noisily, considering the circumstances. But life gives us no training manual for how to behave in moments like this. I watch people give knowing, pity-filled glances to one another and overhear them attempt whispered explanations. Pictures of Linda's happy days—family vacations, birthdays, graduations, and Christmases—cover white poster boards propped on easels. We mourners are detectives, looking for clues in the photographs. *See?*

She's smiling here. Look, here she's smiling again. Someone with that broad and beautiful smile cannot be dead, especially not by her own choosing. Really, there must be a mistake.

I cannot peel my eyes away from one picture taken on Mark and Linda's wedding day. It's a grainy photo of them at their reception, dancing on a makeshift dance floor. He's leaning into her, and she's arching backward, her lithe frame bending easily. Her arms are flung around his neck, and she smiles into his eyes. She's giving herself—all of herself—to him with abandon. Everything about that moment says, "I'm yours! Forever!" He's holding his prize, knowing he doesn't deserve her, but true love is full of grace.

"That's a great picture, isn't it?" Barbara, a fellow parishioner, says behind me.

"Beautiful," I answer, finding it difficult to turn away from Linda's smiling face.

"It's hard to imagine . . . ," Barbara says. She's prodding me, I know it. But I'm not biting. I have nothing to say.

"I know," I say, refusing to look away. I'm not interested in conversation, so Barbara leaves me and heads for the sanctuary. As the pastor's wife, I'm supposed to be comforting and have the right spiritual words to share. But today I'm empty. Even eye contact is asking too much of me at the moment.

I walk through the crowded lobby toward Mark, who is standing next to Linda's casket. I could easily enter the sanctuary without talking to him. I'm sure he doesn't need any more hugs, questions, or hollow condolences. But I press toward him to let him know I care deeply, too.

The untrimmed bearded man in front of me looks a little like

Mark in the same way the shell of a cicada looks like a cicada. "I don't know what to say," he says.

"Hey, Mark, a thousand hugs," I say. I reach up and touch his face with my palm while kissing his opposite cheek. I'm surprised by the softness of his face. In light of the hard realities of the last few days, I would expect him to feel stiff and cold, like marble. Instead he feels soft and warm, his grief palpable and heavy. I hold him to myself for a bit, thinking I might be able to infuse him with some of my strength for the days ahead. Despite his size, he feels light and hollow, like a large silk sheet has taken the shape of a bulky object. I think that if I pulled the silk away, the form beneath might vanish.

"You're a good man," I whisper into his ear.

"Only because she made me that way," he says.

I breathe in and out, hoping he will remember to keep doing the same. When I pull back, I fear the silk might blow away. His likeness remains in front of me, but I can't help but wonder if she's taken him with her. He wrote Linda a letter that will be read at her funeral. In it, he says, "You are not *in* my heart; you *are* my heart." I wonder if his heart will be cremated along with her body.

I take my seat near the back of the sanctuary and listen to the conversations around me. People give audience to stories of pain—their own and others'—at funerals. Everyone is already hurting anyhow, so it's the perfect forum. I'm surrounded by people discussing cancers and gallbladders. One woman discusses Erwin's amputation; another softly giggles about Henry's mole.

The scent of cigarette smoke on mourners' clothes mingles strangely with the scent of funeral flowers. I loathe funeral flowers.

I think they smell like a poor attempt at masking death. I hate that the arrangements are two-dimensional and have flat backs. I'm always shocked that so many people haul their funeral flowers to nursing homes for the residents to "enjoy" when the service is completed. Everyone recognizes a funeral arrangement. Don't the residents take offense?

The organist plays a medley of hymns: "Amazing Grace," "I Come to the Garden Alone," and "It Is Well with My Soul." It's doubtful that this day is well with anyone's soul, but we all try to muster up enough faith to believe that one day things might be well again. When "Rock of Ages" is played, the words echo in my head, "When I close my eyes in death . . . / Rock of Ages cleft for me, / let me hide myself in thee."

I watch the shell of Mark's back as he takes his seat in the front pew. I think he might want to hide himself somewhere this very moment. But where, really, would he find shelter? The storm rages around him, and it appears he has no strength or imagination left to help him find a safe place. Psalm 71:3 meanders through my mind: "Be my strong refuge . . . / You are my rock and my fortress."

I wonder about this as Mark, in front of a few hundred people, battles unspeakable grief. Figuratively, we are all here to help him, but we know that this horrendous struggle is ultimately his and God's alone.

Brad stands to welcome the mourners and lead us through the service. I pray for him, hoping he'll make it through. Although he has a pastor's handbook that outlines funeral services, there's not a section that specifically deals with suicides. Pastors have to figure out most of the tricky, impossible stuff on their own.

Family members and close friends eulogize Linda. She's described as indomitable, creative, and inspirational. They say Linda loved to dance. Her sister says the last time she was with Linda, they danced. The last time.

I wonder if people would end their lives if they knew what would be said about them at their funerals. Would it be possible to choose to leave behind that much love and admiration? What would they think if they looked into the faces of the mourners who line up to say good-bye? Would people abandon their breath if they knew how much pain it would cause?

The service concludes, and we file into the gymnasium for a luncheon. I'm hard-pressed to understand why, exactly, we must eat after a funeral. What is it about saying good-bye to someone we love that makes us want to ingest ham, chicken, pasta, potato salad, and brownies? I join the buffet line in an attempt to be polite and place a few things on my plate that I completely ignore. I head to the plastic-covered banquet tables. Although it's mid-January, Christmas trees still decorate each table. It seems odd, but who cares? These are not ideal circumstances. The tables could be decorated with pumpkins or Easter bunnies. Virtually nothing is appropriate for a luncheon that follows such a tragic, senseless death.

I head for home and wait for Brad to return. It seems I spend a tremendous amount of time waiting for Brad to come home. It's crazy, really. Day after day, I search his eyes and attempt to gauge his heart. I'm especially concerned about what I'll see today because it's been a most impossible day. This life, for some, feels like an impossible life. For Brad, the burden of meeting a person *before* she chooses a horrendous solution is one of the many things that keeps him awake night after night. I wonder where he might find an altar to bring *his* weekly cares. Where can he find a pastor of his own?

When Brad finally walks through the front door, I know something is different. He is visibly relieved that the service is over, but it feels like a piece of him has been removed. Over the next few weeks, he seems more preoccupied and fragile than ever. He sits in the living room and stares at the television set, but he sometimes forgets to turn on the sound. He irons his clothes and fails to unplug the iron. When he climbs into bed, he stares wide-eyed at the ceiling and tosses from side to side, night after night. He waits for sleep to claim him and mercifully give him the rest his body and soul are dying for, but it repeatedly fails to arrive. He seems to be searching for a path that will lead him out of the dark woods and into the sunlit meadow. His very name, Bradley, means "broad meadow." I wish for him to stand in his namesake. Instead, every step leads him into greater darkness.

Frederick Buechner wrote in *Secrets in the Dark*, "Faith is a way of waiting—never quite knowing, never quite hearing or seeing, because in the darkness we are all but a little lost." This is what life feels like these days. We cling to our faith, but we can't seem to navigate through the storm.

I'm a sound sleeper, but I find myself praying for my husband throughout the night. Unrelieved exhaustion is dangerous, and we both know it. Something is broken inside of him, but it's much too deep and too personal to reach. I try to lift him with humor, but he's too buried to respond to my attempts at levity. I cook his favorite foods, but nothing tastes right. I hug him tightly, hoping to squeeze new life into him. I watch him more closely, looking for signs both good and bad. We seem to be waiting for something to change on its own since we no longer know how we might change it ourselves. We're trusting that God will lighten Brad's heart . . . relieve him with rest . . . turn night into day. This has become one of the most difficult waiting places of all.

15

~m~

REFUGE

I am waiting for my husband to be well.

Iquietly enter our bedroom and change into my pajamas in the dark before slipping into bed next to Brad. I try not to make too much noise or rustle the bed any more than necessary. If he is sleeping (which would be a miracle) I don't want to wake him. I position myself carefully, as if Humpty Dumpty himself were sleeping beside me on top of the narrow wall. I listen to his shallow breathing and occasional sighs and know that this will once again be a difficult night. *Oh, God. Please help him sleep. Please.*

It wasn't always this way. Early in our marriage, Brad and I would fall asleep tangled in one another's arms. But that was when

---

he worked in banking, long before his job held eternal consequences. These days, The Church—or now, it seems, *The Church!*—seems to demand more than Brad is able to give. His mistress still whispers in his ear every day and night.

—∿∿—

In addition to conducting multiple funerals, Brad is in the middle of a stressful capital campaign to expand our church's facilities. Church fund-raising is a tricky dance, and it's easy to step on parishioners' delicate feet. While many parishioners express satisfaction with Brad's leadership, others accuse him of failing to follow God. Some people don't like to be asked for money, even for noble purposes. Others, who have experienced or heard of financial abuses in the church, are angry at the mere mention of a campaign. They say, "All the church cares about is money." Still others decide to leave the church because they are appalled that Brad would raise money for a building instead of for charity. The same people who choose to build and maintain their own houses are furious that Brad would want to build and maintain God's house. It's been thirty years since the last renovation, and the congregation has doubled in size, but they argue that the building is fine the way it is.

Some send hurtful notes telling Brad he cares more about buildings than people. Nothing could be further from the truth.

Slowly, sleep is replaced by replaying the day's conversations and mentally rereading the day's scathing e-mails, which he has memorized. Existing without sleep day after day eventually leads to paranoia. He suspects that somebody wants to kill him. He imagines his body sailing through the air, slamming into the wall, and crumpling onto the ground. He tells God it's okay with him if God wants to take him out. In essence, Brad's interested in becoming a modern-day Elijah and would love for God to—*poof!*—beam him up to the clouds. Both Brad and I realize this kind of thinking is dangerous.

Now, lying next to me, Brad turns toward me and presses his forehead into my right shoulder. I curl my right arm around the perimeter of his face and stroke his graying hair with my fingers as he softly cries.

"We'll get some help. Okay, babe?" I say.

Brad nods into my shoulder as tears stream from his exhausted face.

—◊—

The church board decides to send Brad on a three-week guided retreat at Alongside, a Christian counseling center on Gull Lake a few miles from Battle Creek. Ideally, I would be going with him, but it's May, and we have three children who need some stability. They need to go to school. They need help with homework. They need dinner. They need me to stand on the sidelines of their soccer games and sit in the auditoriums for their band concerts. They need me to tuck them in at night, tell them we love them, and wish them sweet dreams.

At their tender ages—twelve, ten, and seven—they need to believe their father simply needs a break. They don't need to know that he also feels like he's being ripped in two. That's too much for any child to handle.

My heart sinks when I learn that Brad is the only one at the retreat center who doesn't have a spouse at his side. Everyone else either has made other arrangements for their kids or, because they homeschool, brought their children along. Brad must wrestle with the monster alone, waiting for his family to visit on weekends.

—⁂—

After a week of single parenting and treading water, I feel like I'm in over my head. The kids don't understand why their dad is gone, and I'm obviously not doing a terrific job of explaining it to them.

"Where's Dad again?" Stephen says, walking into the kitchen where I'm preparing spaghetti.

"He's on a retreat."

"Why?"

"Well, he needs a break," I say, stirring the sauce.

"From us?"

I put the spoon down and face my oldest son, who is so tall he looks me in the eye. "No, not from us. From the church. He has a big job. Sometimes, it's a little more than he can handle. He just needs a rest."

"Maybe he should get a new job."

"Well . . ." This is where it gets tricky. How much do you say to an intuitive twelve-year-old who will call your bluff in a heartbeat? "Maybe he should," I say. "That's something he's trying to figure out."

"I think he'd be a good architect," Stephen says. "He's great at drawing."

"He *is* great at drawing," I say. "But he feels that God has called him to ministry."

Stephen rolls his eyes. "Please, Mom. Do you have to bring God into everything?"

—⁂—

I borrow a friend's GPS, pile the kids into the car, and head for Battle Creek. (A perfect name, I muse, for the town where Brad is fighting for his sanity.) Unfortunately, I'm sick with a kill-me-now cold and fever. There'll be no romance for us this weekend.

Still, although we've been married almost twenty years, I'm as nervous as a schoolgirl when I see him standing outside his temporary residence, a small two-story cottage.

"Hey, babe," I say, accepting a kiss on my fevered cheek. "Sorry I'm sick."

"It's okay. It's okay," he says. There's a gentleness and a vulnerability in his voice that I haven't heard in a while. "Why don't you go lie down?"

The sparsely furnished cottage is outdated but clean. It smells like rotting wood because the dark paneling retains moisture from the lake. I walk up the carpeted stairs, fall into bed, and listen to the kids ooh and ahh about the fabulous "vacation spot" their dad has found for himself. "You're so lucky you get to stay here three whole weeks!" Jordan says.

Oh, to have the innocence of a child. I press my fevered face into a pillow that is not my own, praying that Brad's heart will be lifted.

We spend the weekend riding borrowed bikes, playing on a playground, sitting on the cottage's front porch drinking expensive coffee, and meandering up and down the pebble-stone beach of Gull Lake. If the circumstances were different, this might be beautiful. Instead, it feels fragile. Every word is measured; every action, unnatural, like it's being videotaped. Brad's intensive counseling sessions are helping, but they're peeling away his protective layers, exposing his nerves to the wind. We talk carefully and pick our way through his progress. He talks. I listen.

In bed, I listen to him breathe deeply and feel his body relax for the first time in months, perhaps years. Brad places an arm around me, and we press together as we sleep. *Thank you, God. Please, please help.*

On Sunday, the kids and I repack our things, place them in the car, and say good-bye, knowing we'll be back in five days. As I pull away, Stephen and I fight about the radio station while simultaneously fiddling with the GPS. Later, Brad will tell me that when I failed to wave good-bye one last time, he panicked. All reason temporarily escaped him. All he saw was his family driving away, leaving him behind. He became terrified, convinced we were leaving him for good. He tried to preoccupy himself by heading to the laundry room with his dirty clothes. Amid coin-operated washers and dryers, he cried and prayed and prayed and prayed.

It's tough to know where to turn when your husband's life is falling apart. After all, I can't turn to my pastor; Brad *is* my pastor. If I turn to friends or family members who are church members, will they begin to doubt their pastor and/or church? If I turn to friends or family members who are *not* churchgoers, will they decide to remain outside the doors of the life-giving church (and perhaps the loving arms of God) forever?

Instead, I head to the place that comforts me best—the woods. I walk the worn path and breathe the spring air. I notice the trees putting on their new, bright-green dresses and listen to the way their crinolines brush against each other as they sway in the wind. There, in the midst of the foliage's rebirth, I pray that my husband might experience a renewal of spirit as well.

—⁂—

In order to maintain some semblance of normal, I decide to go to the church's congregational meeting. Gerald, a board member with an enormous heart, is leading the meeting, taking Brad's place. Normally, I like to be inconspicuous at these gatherings and sit near the back. Today, I sit near the front. I want the members to see me. I want them to know everything is all right.

Gerald updates the congregation on the church's budget and capital campaign progress. Other than acknowledging that Brad has asked him to run the meeting, Gerald says little about Brad's whereabouts or the whys surrounding it. Ever the planner, Brad sent a letter out to the congregation informing them of his need for respite before he left. Brad's absence is an elephant in the room. I'm usually the one who likes to point it out. *Hey, look! An elephant!* But today I remain quiet. If I ignore it, perhaps it won't hurt me.

After all business is accounted for, Gerald opens the floor for questions. "Is anybody going to tell us where our pastor is?" Hester, an outspoken member of the congregation, demands.

"Everyone received a letter at the beginning of Pastor's sabbatical," Gerald says.

"I didn't!" Hester says.

"Neither did I!" someone says.

"I didn't get one either," someone else says.

A murmur rattles through the meeting. My stomach turns inside out, and I attempt to shake out the tension in my shoulders without actually moving them. I know my every move is being watched. I feel their eyes on me, searching my nonverbals for what I refuse to say.

Hester continues. "It seems to me that we should know where, exactly, our pastor is and when he's coming back. This isn't a secret society, you know."

"Pastor is at Gull Lake, which is a retreat center for ministers. He's there for rest and recuperation," Gerald says.

"But we know nothing about this Gull Lake. It could be a Baptist camp or a mental institution! You know, the law is on my side."

I have no idea what "law" Hester is talking about, but I suspect it has something to do with the *Free Methodist Book of Discipline*. I remain quiet. I look from Hester to Gerald without wincing or tearing up because I know I'm being watched. I keep my eyes clear and bright. I'm trying to make my face say *everything is fine*.

But everything is not fine. At this very moment, Brad is sitting in circle time with a bunch of other burned-out pastors in need of healing. He's probably nodding sympathetically in response to another's need. Or crying as he pours out his heart. Or laughing with recognition at another's problem. And I'm here, listening to *this*?

In defense of Brad or, perhaps, in defense of myself, I imagine my body sailing through the air and tackling Hester in her pew. The law may be on her side, but I'm thinking of taking it into my own hands.

"I have a question," Jim says from a few pews back. "I've never *heard* of a sabbatical for pastors. Is this going to be a regular thing?"

"Yes, it is," Gerald says. "In fact, the board is figuring out ways for our associate pastor to get away after Brad returns. Are there any more questions?" At this moment, I love Gerald so deeply I could lick his face.

A disgruntled silence hangs in the air as Gerald leads the group in a closing prayer. (There's always a closing prayer, even if there's blood on the pews.) After the meeting, I choose to talk only to friendly faces that don't ask me questions. I collect my children and head for home.

—⁓—

Brad and I talk every day. He fills me in on his counseling progress. He tells me about the struggles of the other pastors and spouses in attendance. It's a relief for both of us to realize his struggle is a shared one. I know he's also working really hard not to turn his experience into a sermon illustration to use on future Sundays. He's trying to keep it between him and God.

When it's time to pile the kids in the car and travel two hours for another weekend visit, I'm downright cantankerous. I've spent the last two weeks hauling kids to karate practice, soccer practice, and soccer games. I've stood alone on sidelines, watching games in the rain. I've sat in auditoriums and listened to my kids perform in band concerts. In addition, I've completed the college course I've been teaching, handed in final grades, met writing deadlines, and driven the neighborhood carpool. I'm worn out. As much as I love Brad, I don't want to travel to visit him for the weekend. I want to *rest*. I don't want to wait for Brad to get better either. I want him to be better *now*.

Mother Teresa once said, "Do not think that love, in order to be genuine, has to be extraordinary. What we need is to love without getting tired." I often wonder how she managed to live that out, given the fact that she chose to live in the mud and muck of life every single day.

Oh, I know God gives us courage. I know he doesn't give us more than we can handle. It's just that sometimes my courage wanes, and I no longer want to wait. Sometimes life and love do end up feeling like a bit more than I can manage. This particular waiting place is crushing me.

Yes, I know God will never leave me or forsake me. I just wish, once in a while, I could feel his hand pressing into my own.

—⁓—

When we arrive for our second weekend together, Brad feels sturdier, and his eyes look a little less bleary. When I squeeze him, I am no longer worried that he might crumble in my arms.

He's excited about the weekend. He knows I've had a busy

two weeks so he's planned and shopped for our meals, which is a brand-new thing for him. He wants to take our family on long bike rides and on walks along the shores of Gull Lake. Most of all, he wants us to take a hike on a wooded trail he's discovered a few miles away.

Things rarely work out the way we imagine them. Since it's early spring in Michigan, Brad's plans are ruined by rain. We wait for it to lift, but the rain remains steady. Friday night is a drizzly gray. Saturday is a complete washout. Brad's anxiety rises. His disappointment with the weekend mingles with his many other disappointments, and I feel him slipping away. *Humpty Dumpty sat on a wall. Humpty Dumpty had a great fall.* I'm trying to figure out how best to catch him.

Perhaps finding the key that will lead us out of the waiting place is dependent on our ability to improvise. We can choose to remain stuck and wait for what might or might not come along, or we can stumble forward in all our imperfections just to see what will come of our efforts.

"Come on. Let's go for a walk anyway," I say. The cottage feels moist and dank. It is depression materialized. This is no place to pass the time.

Brad looks at me blankly. "Babe. It's pouring."

"Maybe it'll lighten up. Besides, it's only rain. We won't melt."

On the drive to the wooded trail, we stop at Walmart for snacks and rain gear. We purchase sushi, bottled water, and a package of Hefty garbage bags. Plastic garbage bags make excellent rain gear in a pinch. They're also a whole lot cheaper than buying five raincoats.

Our family sits in the parking lot that leads to the trail, chomping on sushi, sharing bottled water, and staring at the grayish-white sky. We think we are cool midwesterners because we chose sushi instead of, say, pizza. As the van is pelted by rain, we debate which sushi we like better: shrimp, eel, or California roll. In front of us, the woods are a brilliant green, signifying new life. They beg us to come sloshing in.

We are left with two choices: we can stay in the muggy, fish-smelling van and wait it out indefinitely, or we can risk getting a little wet as we improvise and make the best of what we've been given. We choose the latter. We poke holes into our Heftys so they fit over our heads and arms and—as a family—walk into the woods. Our shoes get muddy. We don't know where we're going. Since this is a foreign place, we don't know what dangers, if any, might lurk in the shadows. Our protection is flimsy but surprisingly sufficient.

In the wet, fragrant air, we take one another's hands and laugh at ourselves. It ain't perfect, but it's enough.

16

DANDELION

I am waiting for my friend to (finally) decide.

My friend Elvera is attentive, generous, and smarter than a room full of Rhodes scholars. She also makes me crazy. This last fact endears her to me all the more.

We are standing in line at Panera Bread at eight thirty on a chilly November Saturday morning. The colorful restaurant is surprisingly quiet, and I am grateful for this small grace. After all, it is going to take Elvera a long time to order. It always does.

Moments ago, she greeted me in the parking lot with a hug. Elvera is not a huggy person, so I gently embrace her petite frame and hold her for as long as she lets me. I am an average-sized woman, but I tower over Elvera. I might as well be Shaquille O'Neill attempting to hug Supreme Court Justice Ruth Bader Ginsburg. I pull away from my former-professor-turned-treasured-friend and look into her penetrating blue eyes.

"Man, it's good to see you, sexy," I say, teasing her.

"Sexy. Yeah, right," she says with a laugh. "It's good to see you, too."

Today, Elvera is wearing her winter burrito—a quilted, gray/lavender puffy coat that wraps her from neck to toe. On her head, she wears a plain black stocking hat that her grown son, Paul, left behind years ago. She probably wears it because she misses him terribly; he and his family now live in Texas. In spite of her insulating getup, Elvera is no doubt freezing. When you're as tiny as she is, it takes more than an oversized parka and a simple knit cap to keep you warm.

She carries a canvas bag filled with students' papers. I've never known her to go anywhere—a conference, a funeral, the bathroom—without a set of papers or journals in need of grading. Manila files stick out of the bag. I figure she's carting around the recent work from three of the six communication classes she's teaching. "What're you gonna do, grade papers while we talk?" I ask.

"Give me a break," Elvera says, growling. "Don't even get me started."

Such is the burden of the committed professor. Tucked into the spaces of everyday life—somewhere between teaching, prepping, working committees, answering telephone calls and e-mails, writing papers for an upcoming conference, and meeting a friend for breakfast—a student's paper is thoughtfully considered. That's not to say her grading is hastily done. In fact, it's safe to say that Elvera sometimes spends more time evaluating papers than her students spend writing them.

Inside Panera, the aroma of freshly baked bread wraps itself around us. Bagels, muffins, and scones are stacked enticingly behind glass. I love this place, and although I don't eat here often, I've memorized the menu. This morning, I want to eat it all, but I'm also trying to cut back and fight off extra midlife pounds that threaten to make me feel like the Stay Puft Marshmallow woman. During the half-hour drive to meet my friend, I decided what I'd order. Sticking with it won't be easy, but I'm determined.

Elvera looks over the choices before us. "So, what're you going to have?"

"A multigrain bagel and coffee," I announce a little too confidently. Like I said, I've thought about this. I intend to stick to my plan.

She looks at me as though I've just announced that I want to ingest laundry lint. "That's all?"

"For now."

Her eyes scan me, landing on my midsection, which I reflexively suck in. "Are you on a diet?"

"No, I'm not on a diet."

"You look like you've lost weight."

"You always say that. Trust me, I haven't lost weight. You just haven't seen me in a while."

Since Elvera lives in New York and I live in Michigan, we don't see each other often. We try to get together when I'm in New York visiting my family, but family takes precedence over friendship.

Our time together never feels like enough, but we make the best of what we have.

"So," she says, continuing to inspect me, "you're not on a diet?"

"Nope."

"Then why aren't you eating more?"

"I will."

"When?"

"Later. Oh my gosh, stop being such a pain."

"Humph." She looks me over again. "Well, if you're not going to eat anything, I'm not going to order something big."

Here we go. "Elvera, order what you want. It's eight thirty in the morning. I don't eat a lot in the morning."

"So you skip breakfast regularly?" she says accusingly. Her eyes meet mine, and I force myself to hold her gaze with my own. I know her stare so well. It's the same one she gives her students when she asks who has read the assigned chapter. Students don't have the audacity to lie to her. They know she'll immediately call them out.

"How am I skipping breakfast?" I say. "That bagel is the size of a small child!"

She ignores my attempt at humor, squinting at the menu printed on the wall. A college-aged employee whose nametag reads "Amanda" waits for us to step forward and place our order. She's wearing a green apron and a baffled expression. As she shifts her weight from foot to foot, I suspect she's thinking, *What is* wrong *with these women? It's breakfast, not a new car.*

"This is normal," I tell the cashier. "We're like this everywhere we go."

Amanda nods, but her smile is tinged with bewilderment. I often get this look when I'm with Elvera. We have mutual friends who marvel at our friendship, and I've heard it said, "You just can't find two people who are more different." I don't care. I secretly love that nothing is easy with her. I'll wait for her as long as it takes.

Truth be told, I'd rather be visiting Elvera in her home right now instead of in Panera. She doesn't like to have people in her house because she says it's such a mess. But I don't see her "messes." Instead, the things that fill it are meaningful extensions of my enormously complicated friend. Where she sees piles of papers ready to topple over in her kitchen, I see the students' work that she has valued enough to keep. Where she sees countertops that require dusting, I see treasured collections carefully displayed. Where she sees old furniture, blankets, and rugs, I see objects eroded beautifully—like beach glass—over the span of time.

If I could give someone a tour of her home, I'd say, "Look! Here's a rug worn thin by the pacing of a mother as she attempted to get her child to sleep . . . and here's a couch worn out by a professor who sits and reads thousands of papers written by students who clumsily interpret her favorite theorists . . . and here's a piano sitting dusty and silent, wishing to be played by the beloved son who is now a professor, husband, and dad, living fourteen hundred miles away."

I'd then walk over to her bookshelf and pick up my favorite object: a single dandelion flower encased in acrylic. Through the plastic, I see a flower that has gone to seed and is sporting its full-on white Afro. Most people would not appreciate its beauty. After all, isn't every dandelion a nuisance? But the dandelion—like Elvera herself—begs the question, "What is beauty?"

Like a dandelion, Elvera tends to pop up in unexpected places. I've watched as others have treated her as a bothersome weed. But those who take the time to understand her know that she's gentle, fair, and resilient. Problem is, few want to take the time.

Most remarkable about the dandelion artifact is that, as the artist poured the acrylic around the flower's head, a single seed broke free. The individual puff of white is suspended apart from the homogenous crowd, ready to plant itself elsewhere. The seed reminds me of Elvera: distinctive . . . singularly lovely . . . and poised to wreak havoc in an otherwise uniform field.

Whenever I hold the dandelion in my hand—or embrace Elvera in my arms—I am reminded to breathe a word of thanks.

———

In Panera, Elvera continues to consider the many choices before us. "Oh, I don't know if I want a breakfast sandwich or something sweet."

"You're joking, right? Get something sweet. You *always* want something sweet."

"I know, but I'm thinking about something more substantial. Maybe I'll get something sweet later."

"Why don't you get both right now so we can sit down?"

"Because I don't know what I want," she says, exasperated.

An elderly couple enters the restaurant, and I tell them to go in front of us. "Really, go ahead. We're still deciding." They look at us, unsure, but shuffle to the counter. Amanda looks relieved to be able to wait on people who actually know what they want.

———

I take a deep breath, cross my arms, and resume waiting as Elvera continues to stew. We both know she'll end up regretting whatever she orders, wishing she would have chosen the better thing. Still, I love Elvera. I will gladly wait until she selects her breakfast or until hell freezes over, whichever comes first. After all, I owe her a piece of my life.

Elvera-the-professor introduced me to Parker Palmer, Kenneth Burke, and Rainer Maria Rilke. Elvera-the-friend introduced me to Bach, broccoli, and Häagen-Dazs Rum Raisin ice cream. (I still don't love broccoli or Bach, but Rum Raisin rocks!)

Over home-cooked meals in her and her husband's home, she taught me the words to the dinner blessing, "Come, Lord Jesus, be our guest. Let these gifts to us be blessed." Singlehandedly, this woman took an energetic girl who listened to classic rock and transformed her into a woman who is utterly addicted to NPR.

She believed in my spunk and curiosity and thought I might make a good teacher. She wrote recommendations to graduate schools and employers. (To our continual dismay, it was her recommendation that was misplaced when I applied to the PhD program.) Today, I teach and write, in part, because of her profound influence. Following her example, I try to ask my students the hard questions and wait quietly for the truest answers. I've found that, when I'm willing to wait, thoughtful responses eventually show up in good discussions, and we all learn from them. Patience truly is rewarded. I've never stopped being surprised by that.

Perhaps most intriguing is the fact that I find myself unconsciously mimicking Elvera's listening position when I'm leading a classroom discussion. As I wait for a student to work through his or her profundity, I stand with my left arm crossed in front of me, right elbow resting on the back of my left hand, right finger curled like a question mark around my lips, head tilted downward, eye contact full-on, eyebrows raised. When I "assume the position" I am no longer Eileen, but Elvera. Teaching is hard. Channeling her gives me courage.

Whatever Elvera has given me in mind, she has given me doubly in heart. When Brad's dark night of the soul threatened to rip him—and us—apart, Elvera called me on the phone and listened even when I could not speak the words. That summer, she boarded a plane and flew to Michigan to be with me a while. During her visit, we didn't dwell on the year's difficulties. Instead we talked about teaching and students and ice cream and poetry. That was more than enough. Her decision to fly to my neck of the woods reminds me of an exchange from A. A. Milne's *Winnie-the-Pooh*:

> Piglet sidled up to Pooh from behind. "Pooh?" he whispered.
>
> "Yes, Piglet?"
>
> "Nothing," said Piglet, taking Pooh's hand. "I just wanted to be sure of you."

This, I think, is the truest definition of friendship.

"I think I might want a breakfast sandwich," Elvera finally says.

"Okay. Get one."

"Oh, I just don't know. Do you think they put onions on their breakfast sandwiches?"

I turn to the glassy-eyed cashier. "Are there onions in the breakfast sandwiches?"

"Hey, Tony!" she calls out. "You put onions on the breakfast sandwiches?"

"Only if they want 'em."

"Nope," she says, turning back to us. "Only if you want them." (Tony stands waiting for our order with his metal spatula gripped tightly. If Tony were the *Seinfeld* Soup Nazi, we would have been thrown out long ago.)

"I can't stand onions," Elvera says to the air.

"Or chocolate . . . or nuts . . . or garlic. My word, you are high maintenance, you know that?"

"Don't start."

I'm struck with a bolt of genius. "Hey! They have a spinach artichoke spread for lunch sandwiches. Maybe they could put it on your egg and cheese."

It's risky to introduce a new idea to this already difficult process, but it's one worth taking. It might actually get us into a booth and a conversation before lunchtime.

"Spinach artichoke? Where do you see that?" she says, squinting again at the menu board.

"It's on the lunch menu, but I bet they could . . ." I turn to Amanda, who now hates me with a fiery passion, and ask, "Do you think we can have the spinach artichoke spread on an egg and cheese?"

She's ready to sell us the restaurant if it will get us out of her face. "Tony!" she hollers again. "Can you put some spinach artichoke on an egg and cheese?"

Tony is good-natured about it and shrugs. "Don't see why not."

"Yep," Amanda says. "No problem."

"So you're getting a sandwich now?" Elvera says to me.

"Wha—?"

"A sandwich. You're getting a breakfast sandwich?" she asks.

I cannot believe it. She's done it again. "Sure," I say with a smile and shrug. "Why not?"

—⁓—

We are exceedingly blessed if we have friends who are willing to stand next to us in the waiting place. Friends who ask questions and listen for the authentic (and sometimes ugly) answers make the best life companions. Elvera is that to me. We may not be the same age, share the same tastes, or have much of anything in common. People who treasure a friendship like this understand the depth and flavor it adds to their lives. Without it, life would be shallow and vanilla at best.

17

—◆—

WINDBLOWN TAILS

I am waiting for my children to grow up.

All three kids are crawling around the kitchen like spiders. Stephen is on the bench seat, Kristina is on top of the kitchen counter, and Jordan is about to slide off the top of the fridge. They are laughing and shouting instructions to each other.

"What're you guys doing?"

"It's a contest, Mom," Stephen says as he climbs from the bench to the top of a stand-alone cabinet. "We have to go around the kitchen without touching the floor."

I remember this game. It's a blast when you're a kid. But momhood has given me a new definition of "fun." Especially when I look at Jordan's dirty feet and realize there will be footprints on top of the fridge.

"Well, can you do this somewhere else? I need to make dinner."

"Hold on, Mom. We have to finish first," Stephen says.

Jordan descends from the fridge and asks, "What's for dinner?"

"Spaghetti."

"Aw, I don't like spaghetti."

"Yeah? Too bad."

"Can I have cereal instead?"

"Nope. It's spaghetti or nothin'."

"Aw, man!"

I watch my Spiderboys and Spidergirl make their way around the perimeter safely. I get the cleanser out from under the sink and proceed to spray the counters as I listen to them fight over who won the contest. Since they're now banished from the kitchen, they decide to take turns climbing the doorway instead. With their bodies in the shape of Xs, they shimmy up the doorjambs until their heads touch the ceiling. I turn on the stove burner as I jot a mental note to clean the footprints off the walls.

While they take turns scaling the doorway, I take the large pot from my disorganized cupboard and fill it with water. I've boiled a pound of spaghetti at least one night a week for the past twenty years. According to my calculations, this means I've cooked over a thousand pounds of pasta. I wonder what a thousand pounds of cooked pasta looks like. Would it fill my living room? My house? As I plunge the stiff strands into the boiling water, I try to locate my gratitude for this cheap, easy meal.

It's a good thing I like making dinner or this would be the

worst time of day. I tend to love people with food, even if it's a simple pot of generic spaghetti with cheap canned sauce poured on top. I don't knit, scrapbook, or needlepoint, so making dinner is the craftiest thing I do. It's creative, it's pleasing to the eye, and I don't have to figure out where to display it once it's made.

If I am perfectly honest, making dinner is more than creative "me time." It has also helped me escape from having to play with my kids. Over the years, having to sauté onions, mash potatoes, and debone chickens has freed me from some tortuous alternatives. Consider these exchanges:

Ten years ago . . .

Stephen: "You wanna play LEGOs with me, Mommy?"

Me: "Oh, honey, I'd love to, but I have to make dinner."

Five years ago . . .

Kristina: "Mama, can you play Barbies with me?"

Me: "Sorry, babe. Gotta make dinner."

This year . . .

Jordan: "Hey, Ma. Check out this YouTube video."

Me: "Can't. Dinner."

Having to make dinner has saved me from having to spend precious hours of my life playing LEGOs, Trouble, and Monopoly. I'd rather be cooking just about anything than playing a poke-my-eyes-out board game. Sometimes I feel a little guilty about begging off on a game of Go Fish!, but the feeling only lasts as long as it takes me to say, "Who wants chocolate cake?"

"Me!" they happily respond in unison.

Smiling, I pull the sugar, flour, and cocoa from the cupboard, knowing I've managed to slip off the hook again.

My mom used to joke that she had three kids so she could have enough helpers to do the dishes. "I have a washer, a dryer, and a putter-away-er," she'd say, laughing. With hands wrinkling in soapy water and a dish towel flung over our shoulders, my sisters and I didn't think that was very funny. Likewise, I joke that I had three kids so they'd have built-in playmates. I've admitted to friends, "I had three so I'd never have to play Candy Land." My kids have yet to laugh along.

It's early morning, and I'm getting ready for the day when Brad lumbers into the bathroom and sits down. He sighs heavily as he places his head in his hands.

"How was your sleep?" I ask.

He sighs again. "Fine."

Liar.

One look in the mirror tells me that Brad and I barely resemble the grab-life-by-the-horns kinda people we set out to become. We look middle-aged, puffy, and tired. We have battled life together and have our share of scars. To lighten the moment, I serenade him with my imitation of Jon Foreman, the lead singer of the band Switchfoot: "This is your life, are you who you want to be / This is your life, is it everything you dreamed that it would be / When the world was younger and you had everything to lose."

"Humph," Brad says. "Not funny."

The bathroom counter is littered with toiletries, used Q-tips, nail clippers, and random puddles of water, mouthwash, and saline solution. The mirror is speckled with the spew from someone's sloppy tooth-brushing habits. And the floor is sprinkled with . . . well, we really don't want to know *what* that is.

"Someday, Eileen. Someday. When the kids are grown up . . ."

"Don't wish it away," I interject, but we both sigh in unison. After all, there are things we'd like to do. Freedoms we'd like to experience. Places we'd like to go. (*Oh, the places we'd like to go!*) Neither of us wants to rush time, but we want to make love without wondering if the kids can hear us. We'd like to live in a smaller home that doesn't look like a grenade exploded in it. We envision clutter-free spaces devoid of school papers, pop bottle collections, plastic transforming toys, Pokemon cards, and Disney movies. We want to spend a quiet evening together without having to scream, "Turn that music down!"

Given our life stage, these are selfish things to want, and we both know it. Still, we wish and wait for them, in spite of our guilt.

—⁓—

In a rare moment of peace, Brad and I are sitting side by side on our front porch. I am reading a fabulous novel. Brad is reading a book about church leadership, which is what he does for fun. It's a beautiful summer evening, and we plan to spend the next few hours glued to these chairs.

The kids are playing throughout our neighborhood. Stephen is on a neighbor's porch, discussing the pros and cons of Xbox versus PlayStation. Jordan and Kristina race the kids across the street. I peek up over my book long enough to marvel at Kristina's long legs and the way her brown hair folds over itself in the wind as she runs. I am awed by Jordan, who takes off like Speedy Gonzales. I try to never take that grace for granted. I think back to the day when we didn't know if he would ever walk, let alone run. The fact that he's as strong, fast, and athletic as he is now is nothing short of a miracle.

The kids get bored with their conversation and games and decide to take me on. Suddenly, they're standing in front of me like a posse. "Let's go fly a kite, Mom," Kristina says.

"Yeah. Come on," Jordan adds. "Please?"

I look at Brad and he burrows deeper into his book. Today, he's no help whatsoever. I look back at my children, who are a determined bunch. Stephen has his arms crossed before him, feet spread apart, head tilted to one side. He's daring me, I know it. He has known me the longest, so he believes I'll think of an excuse not to do this. Since we've already eaten dinner, he knows I can't escape to my pots and pans. Neither can I blame the rain (there isn't any), the lack of wind (there's a perfect breeze in the air), the heat (it's about seventy degrees), or the night (sunset is a full two hours away). I'm tempted to distract them with, "Who wants chocolate chip cookies?" But I don't.

I look into his eyes and realize that I've begged off a few times too often. He doesn't trust me to say yes to their childhood games. It really doesn't matter that I feed/clothe/carpool/hug/love my kids. They want me to *play*. They want me to run, leap, and laugh with them. They want me to forget my boring book and my boring adulthood and try, on this night, to be one of the kids.

Stephen's eyes tell me there will soon come a day when he will outgrow his desire to fly kites with his mom. It's time for me to suck it up and play.

"Okay," I say, closing my book and peeling my rear out of my worn wicker chair. "Let's go."

"Really?" Kristina says.

"Really. It'll be fun."

They can hardly believe it as they scurry into the garage to find the kite. They're quick about it because they don't want to miss this small window of opportunity. They know the phone could ring or a friend could pull into the driveway to divert my intention to play with them. They're not about to lose this chance.

We walk toward the cool wooded trail behind our subdivision. It winds through trees and over streams and tumbles out into an open field. As the four of us enter the deep, green woods, I try to remember why we don't do this every single night. It's fragrant with leaves, pine, and wildflowers. As we walk, we discuss everything and nothing.

We get to the open field, and the kids take turns running up and down the manmade hill that's been created in the middle of it. We live in a very flat part of Michigan. The peak of the two-story hill is probably the highest point in our town.

On top of the mound, Stephen unravels the kite and prepares to fly it. I've never flown a kite before so I'm no help, which is a good thing for my oldest son, who is much better at intuitively figuring out how things work than I am. He runs down the hill with the kite behind him, and together we watch as it climbs into the clouds.

It's funny how proud flying a kite can make you feel. Watching the splash of color dance against the backdrop of blue and white is surprisingly exhilarating. I can't believe I've waited this long to experience it.

Stephen concentrates on flying the kite higher into the sky. He'd like it to touch a cloud. Kristina lingers near Stephen and me while Jordan, who has quickly tired of our game, runs down the hill at full speed. I look at my children—my amazing, exasperating, wonderful children—and tuck the memory of them at this moment into my heart.

"Thanks, Mom," Kristina says. "This is awesome."

"You're welcome. It *is* pretty awesome, isn't it?"

"Yeah," she says, looking up at the kite. "It's like fishing in heaven." She takes off, running after Jordan. "I'll race you, Jordan!" she yells.

My breath is sucked away, and time stands still. *Fishing in heaven.* That's what I would have missed on this perfect evening had I chosen to remain on the porch and click off the hours till bedtime. I would have missed that the kids are getting taller and wiser. I would have missed the chance to laugh and play. I would have missed the sacred moment when we realized we were not merely flying a kite but fishing the divine skies.

Life often feels like we're fishing in heaven. We cast into the universe and wonder where God is in the midst of it all. We peer through the hairballs of everyday life in hopes that God himself might take our hand. Even the most faithful people stumble over their too-large feet as they traipse through the muck, praying all the while to be lifted from it. We all want to glimpse the divine.

When I finally decide to step outside my psyche and pry open my squinty eyes, I realize that I am surrounded by exquisite art-istry: The look of wonder on my children's faces. Their ability to run and roll in the grass. The sound of their unrestrained laughter. These marvelous moments are mine for the noticing.

We can wait all our lives for the next stage to come. Or we can choose to see the waiting place for what it often is: unexpectedly magical and holy.

18

※

WIGMOM

I am waiting for my mother to accept me.

The Hallmark store is filled with anxious card hunters. Most of them are women. (Which leaves me wondering where the men are hiding. Don't they have mothers, too?) Together, we card hunters do the Mother's Day Card Dance. We take turns reaching for, reading, and putting back hundreds of sentiments, hoping to find the perfect one.

I pull a pink and white one from its slot. It reads, "Mom, love is what I see in all the things you've done for me."

Blech.

Another reads, "A mother is someone whose capacity for giving is as limitless as the sky."

Oh, please.

I turn toward the serious-looking woman standing beside me. "This shouldn't be this hard, should it?" I ask. She smiles weakly and continues to dance. I fall in step, now with greater focus. *Come on, Eileen. It's a Mother's Day card, not a wedding dress. It doesn't have to be perfect. Just pick one already.*

Here's the problem: I'm quite aware that my mom prefers to receive meaningful cards with lovely, appreciative phrases written by poets like Helen Steiner Rice. She desires a sentiment that will bring tears to her eyes and assurance to her heart. A pastel piece of paper that reads, in gold scripted letters, "Mom, you are my world . . . my universe . . . my life!"

But I can't send her a card like that. It feels phony. Plastic. The fact that I'm naturally drawn to cards that feature potty humor doesn't help. I also like cards that begin with the words like, "Do your boobs hang low, do they wobble to and fro', can you tie 'em in a knot, can you tie 'em in a bow?"

Unfortunately, Helen Steiner Rice doesn't write Mother's Day cards about potty habits. Or boobs. So I pick, read, grimace, and replace. Pick, read, grimace, and replace. It's a good thing I've got some time to kill. This is going to take awhile.

—⟋⟍—

When I was a kid, Mom was the melody and I was the harmony. Then I grew up and developed tastes of my own (strange as they are). Today, Mom and I are as different as opera and hip-hop. Our differences extend light-years beyond our taste in greeting cards.

For instance, consider our clothing. Mom wears sequins, sparkles, and animal prints purchased primarily from QVC and the Home Shopping Network. Every clothing item has its own colorful, coordinating ensemble: shoes, handbags, belts, jewelry, hats. She is Zsa Zsa Gabor meets Lucille Ball meets Peg Bundy. Really. My tastes run toward cotton and denim primarily purchased from T.J.Maxx and Target. My entire wardrobe is grounded in three noncolors: black, white, and brown.

Mom's wardrobe is housed in overstuffed closets, dozens of large plastic containers, and a rented storage unit. My entire wardrobe could fit, with room to spare, into three Rubbermaid eighteen-gallon containers. Mom rotates her clothes and accessories according to the seasons, but I can't be bothered with seasonal wear. The T-shirt I wear in June is the same T-shirt I wear in December.

Mom adores jewelry and owns several boxes stuffed with inexpensive baubles. As odd as it sounds, I think most jewelry is unnecessary. I'm missing the bauble gene; I just don't like it. I keep my entire collection sorted in a single ice-cube tray in my dresser drawer.

Mom turns heads when she pumps gas or shops for groceries because she is always dressed to the nines. I turn heads while shopping at Home Depot or Lowe's because I'm often covered in dirt or paint. If Mom ran into me in public, it might take her awhile to recognize me.

Mom likes stuff: life-size dolls, Precious Moments figurines, dancing Santas, and Princess Diana paraphernalia. She loves ornately decorated rooms that feature crystal chandeliers and gold accents. I study voluntary simplicity (for fun!) and am a minimalist at heart. I'm most comfortable in rooms that are colorful but primarily empty.

Mom prefers gold, surf and turf, Neil Diamond, and her red, sporty American-made car. I prefer silver, pizza, classic rock, and twenty-year-old Hondas.

Mom's dream vacation includes a cruise to an exotic location featuring an all-you-can-eat buffet. Mine is a rustic cabin in the woods featuring a nearby fruit and vegetable stand. Mom lives with a wonderful man who regularly takes her on cruises and makes her vacation dreams come true. I try to show interest in their excursions, but it's not easy.

"I don't think I could ever go on a cruise," I say.

"Why not? They're maar-velous!" she purrs.

"I don't know. It's just . . ." I don't want to hurt her feelings. Although there may come a day when I eat my words, cruises go against just about everything I believe in. All the money, entertainment, and twenty-four-hour, all-you-can-eat buffets gross me out. When I ask myself, *What would Jesus do?* I can't imagine him answering, "Go on a cruise!"

"It's just . . . Well, there are so many people in the world who have nothing. I don't know if I could enjoy a cruise."

"Let me ask you something, Eileen," Mom says. She is very serious. She's giving me her Dr. Phil imitation, looking me directly in the eye. "Do rich people intimidate you?"

"Wha—?"

"Because rich people put their pants on one leg at a time just like we do. There's no reason to be intimidated by them."

I just don't know what to say. It's tough to win when we seem to be playing different games.

Perhaps the greatest difference between my mom and me is evident in our hair. (Because, you know, it's all about the hair.) My mother is a blonde who spends hours getting ready in the morning. People tell her that her hair always looks perfect because it always does. In fact, I have never seen my mother in public with a single hair out of place. I'm convinced that she single-handedly keeps hairspray manufacturers in business.

In the past few years, Mom has started wearing big, blonde wigs—the kind that might make Phyllis Diller a little jealous. When Mom is feeling especially festive, she attaches curly pony-tails to the wigs. She dramatically drapes them over her shoulders, poufs them, and sprays them into place. Often, she tops it all off with a pinned-on hat.

It can be quite a surprise to see a New Yorker sporting a big, blonde wig complete with attachments. I've watched passersby suffer whiplash in their attempt to get a second look at her. The extra attention has never bothered my mother. In fact, she loves it. It seems to inspire her. And gosh darn it, you have to admire a woman whose personal philosophy boils down to the simple phrase: Life is short. Wear the pigtails.

Much to my mother's dismay, I am a brunette who insists on wearing her own boring hair. My idea of the perfect hairstyle is one that can be done in three minutes or less. When I'm in an especially festive mood, I look . . . well, exactly the same. My weapon of choice is a flat iron. Once in a while, I use a little pomade to smooth down my cowlicks. And since I can't be bothered to keep up with my "natural highlights" (ahem!), I regularly sport a lovely gray "skunk stripe" in between color jobs, which I do myself. I buy my color (Garnier Medium Golden Brown) on sale at Rite-Aid for $4.99.

I'm a little too proud of the fact that I can shower, dress, and face the world in twelve minutes flat. I'm what you might call "low maintenance." I once boasted to my sister Susie that I could put on my makeup without looking in a mirror.

"Are you bragging about that, Eileen? Because I'm thinking that's not something you should be bragging about," she said.

Basically, I run around looking a little like Bon Jovi. It drives my Zsa Zsa mother wild.

It's been thirty years since my mother styled my hair. Amazingly, she's still trying to do it.

"Eileen. Come here," my mother says, motioning for me to join her in my sister's bathroom. I brace myself. I can tell from the tone of her voice that she wants to take me somewhere I don't want to go.

"Just a second," I say, turning to Susie, who is casually sautéing onions in a frying pan. "Uh-oh." I reach for her glass of merlot and take a gulp. I don't like merlot. It tastes like dirt. But I need the fortification. Susie, who is nicely relaxed from the wine, laughs quietly.

Mom, otherwise known as the most intuitive person in the universe, senses my reluctance. "Oh, just come here," she says playfully.

I breathe in and out as I walk fifteen strides to my sister's bathroom.

"Yeah?" I say. There's a tremor in my voice. My eyes dart around the small room, looking for what Mom will show me. I remind myself to breathe.

"I have something for you," she says as she reaches into a used plastic bag. She pulls out a blonde, short-haired wig.

I quickly scan the room again, now looking for the hidden camera.

"I want you to try this on. I think it would look great on you," she says.

"Mom. No."

"Oh, stop it."

"It's a wig!" *Please tell me this is a joke.* I search her eyes, but she's serious about her attempt to perform an *Extreme Makeover: Hair Edition* on me.

"But it's your style," she says as she attempts to hand it to me.

I back away from the wig like it's a possum. "If it's my style, why would I need a wig?"

"Come on. Just try it."

She means well. I get defensive anyway. "No, Mom. Absolutely not."

"But it would look adorable on you," she says dejectedly. I hear the little voice in my head tell me, *It's no big deal, Eileen. Just try it on. No one will see you. Besides, it will make her happy for a minute. Just do it.*

I tell the little voice in my head to shut up.

"Nope. Sorry, Mom, you've crossed a line. I just can't wear a wig." I walk back toward my sister and try to catch her eye. Susie doesn't look back at me; she's pretending to focus on dinner.

Suddenly she's sautéing with the fury of Emeril Lagasse. I don't know whether to laugh or cry. I reach again for her merlot and take another gulp as I hear Mom put the wig back in the plastic bag.

Mom is hurt. After all, she's just trying to make me "pretty." But I'm hurt, too. I hear the echo of the counseling session we attended together when I was in my early twenties. At the time, I was working through the disappointment and guilt I felt over my parents' divorce, along with the perfection trap I had managed to fall into along the way. I wanted my mother to accept me as a separate person rather than an extension of herself. I wanted her to be able to say she loved me for who I was on my own terms.

Carol, my counselor, was patient and methodical. She helped me pick my way through the minefield as she listened, asked questions, and handed me tissues. During the sit-down with my mother, Carol worked hard to get to the root of the problem between us.

"Bonnie," Carol said, "do you love your daughter?"

"Of course I do," Mom said, obviously insulted by the question. "It's just that she could be such a pretty girl."

My mother sat tall in her blouse, skirt, high heels, and stockings. Her perfectly manicured hands, nails painted bright red, lay crossed on her knee. She maintained eye contact and a pleasant smile with just a little lipstick covering the tips of her teeth. She blinked beautifully at Carol while I, in my white T-shirt, jeans, and sneakers, felt the knife twist in my heart.

I could be such a pretty girl.

Those words, so innocently spoken, rise up in me like a Whac-A-Mole that refuses to die. Sometimes I take my imaginary rubber mallet and bash them down. I tell them they were said long ago. I tell them they don't matter anymore. But they repeatedly pop up their ugly little heads in unexpected places. Since the game is cruel to both Mom and me, I wonder why I still play it. An even bigger question is this: what words will I say about my own daughter that she will have to repeatedly bash down in the years ahead of us?

It's difficult to find the silver lining in this waiting place since it's created through our repeated attempts to change one another. We're so different that we've forgotten how to lean in and appreciate the other for who she is. If we weren't mother and daughter, we might be great friends. But the mother-daughter relationship is one of the trickiest. It demands flexibility, love, and unconditional acceptance. When those things are in short supply, we end up dancing clumsily with one another and stepping on each other's toes. It would be good for both of us to try a little harder to learn the other's dance.

As we stumble through our years together, Mom and I continue to seek common ground. Sometimes it feels like we might have to wait until halfway through eternity before we discover it.

And yet . . .

If I'm willing to admit it, my mom and I are alike in many of the ways that matter the most. For instance, my mom's laugh is loud and bursts from her unexpectedly. As a child, I was mortified when I could hear her guffaw in a crowded place. Today, I often hear the same unrestrained laughter coming from myself. Once in a while, I catch my children rolling their eyes when they hear me burst into a giggling fit. It's a look that says, *That's my mom. She's so embarrassing!* And I realize in those moments that Mom and I are both able to find terrific joy in surprising places.

Also, Mom is an amazing listener. She has a wonderful gift for making a person feel that he or she is the most fascinating person to ever grace the planet. I've watched Mom listen to an elderly man describe, with explicit detail, his gallbladder surgery. No doubt, she wanted to escape or at least shout in frustration, "Listen, man, you are so much more than your gallbladder!" But she didn't. Instead, with a concerned look on her face, she asked questions and sighed, shaking her head compassionately. When parishioners stop me in the church narthex to tell me about their colonoscopies or sinus infections, I conjure up images of my mother and try to imitate her compassion. Mom might live six hours away, but she helps me stop whirling long enough to give others my undivided attention.

Perhaps most importantly, my mother loves my sisters and me with her entire being. I love my kids the exact same way.

—ɷ—

In my mind's eye, I see her. She's walking into the gym to sit on the hard, unforgiving bleachers to watch my gymnastics meet. She's genuflecting at St. Jerome's Catholic Church, where I am being confirmed. She's entering the high school auditorium to listen to me scrape through the "Hallelujah Chorus." She's sitting on folding chairs as I receive my high school and college diplomas.

Time and time again, I look into the crowd and find her immediately. I simply scan the audience until I spot her big, blonde hair that shines like a beacon in the night. I wave, and she shoots me a smile that is filled with optimistic anticipation, love, and encouragement. It's all I need to be my best self.

Ours may be a complicated relationship, and we may not understand one another's choices or preferences, but Mom is one of my biggest fans. She believes in me. Always has.

I only hope my kids can say the same of me.

I haven't always appreciated the ways Mom has expressed her love for me. It's quite possible that she will always want to style my hair. She might always hope to find in me a little less Bon Jovi and a little more Zsa Zsa Gabor. She might always wish I would try to be a little more presentable in public. But when I reframe her suggestions in love, rather than disappointment, I am able to accept them—and her—with a more open heart.

And while it usually takes many hours, most years I'm able to find a Mother's Day card that bridges our great divide.

19

---m---

UNCLE TOM

I am waiting for my godfather to take his last breath.

By the time I arrive at my uncle Tom's bedside, he is no longer conscious. "Hi, Uncle Tom," I say, touching his shoulder. "It's Eileen." I move in close to his face to kiss him on the cheek. Uncle Tom is five years older than my dad. Like many siblings, they look a lot alike. Given the present circumstances, the resemblance sends a chill down my spine.

I smile into his face, but his mouth is slack, and his half-open eyes register no recognition. If I had arrived a day earlier, I would have seen him awake. Perhaps I would have been able to talk to him. To say good-bye. At least then he would have known that his goddaughter was here.

Oh, how I am regretting Brad's and my decision to move to Michigan. We are so far away from my family. I hate this, but it's a sign of the times. Most families have at least one loved one who lives far away. In our culture we no longer have to figure out how to live daily life together. Instead, we schedule visits for holidays and special occasions. When the Gables gather, it's for wedding showers and baby showers. We celebrate by eating kielbasa and golumpkies. We polka together at weddings and cry together at funerals. We arrive in time to watch each other take last breaths.

If only I had gotten here sooner.

Like my dad, my uncle Tom is a simple man who enjoys simple pleasures. He loves his family, the Catholic Church, Mother Mary, and a good cup of coffee with seven teaspoons of sugar. He's always on the lookout for a good story or joke and likes to repeat them with lengthy embellishments. In his world, there's no such thing as a short story. Each one is Tolstoyian in length. If he wants to tell a group of people about something he heard on the news, for instance, he begins by explaining what he ate for breakfast.

His face is very expressive: he has a large nose, wide-set eyes, and distinctly pointed eyebrows that look like they might be drawn on. It's impossible not to laugh when he tells a joke, not because he's such a fabulous joke teller, but because of his delighted expression when he finally reaches the punch line.

Today, I'd like him to open his eyes and tell me something. I'd like to be able to laugh with him once more.

Instead, I'll have to live vicariously through my sister Susie.

Just a few days ago, she visited Uncle Tom and talked with him as he was propped up in his hospice bed. He was animated, but he knew he was dying.

"I have to tell you something, Susie," he said.

Susie braced herself. Uncle Tom has always had a flair for the dramatic.

"My casket is blue. I'm a blue guy."

"Okay," she said, laughing a little.

"And I want them to put my hands like this," he said, placing his hands apart on his stomach. "It's more natural. I hate it when they fold them like this," he said, crisscrossing them. "Who sleeps with their hands folded like that?"

"I don't know. I like to sleep on my stomach," Susie said, although she had yet to attend a wake where the body lay prostrate in the casket.

"And I don't want them to put me in a suit and tie," he said. He squinted his eyes and wagged his finger as if scolding. "They're not gonna bury me with a noose around my neck!" He folded his hands in his lap, straightened up, and nodded his head as if to say, *So there!*

He went on to say that he had just installed a new toilet in his downstairs bathroom. "I'm just sad that I'm not going to get to use it," he said, sighing. Susie didn't know whether to laugh or cry.

—⁂—

It's late and I'm at my dad's place, editing my weekly newspaper column. The mobile home is old and worn but comfortable—like a favorite slipper. I often wish I could afford to buy Dad a "real" house, but he's content to live in these paneled walls. If he isn't, he would never tell me. Both my parents make the best of their circumstances. It's a trait I admire and try to imitate in my own life, although it's not always easy.

I work as quietly as I can, because Dad is sleeping on the couch behind me. He's exhausted. He has stayed at the hospital throughout the night for the past five nights. In the dimly lit hospital room, Dad watches his brother breathe. Tonight, I watch my father breathe. I can hardly imagine the excruciating pain that Uncle Tom's daughters must be experiencing. Any day now, they will lose their dad, and I will keep mine—for as long as God allows. My gratefulness is mingled with guilt.

My dad might be seventy-three, but he looks like a child sleeping here. He's wrapped from neck to toes in a pink, fuzzy blanket. His head rests on a pillowcase covered in irises. He has removed his dentures, and his mouth is slightly open. Moments from now, his deep breathing will become a full-blown snorefest, and I will have to suppress my giggles. I shouldn't be sneaking peeks at him anyway. I should be writing. But it's difficult to work when your dad is so beautiful, vulnerable, strong, and alive before you. It's tough to care about deadlines when life hangs in its precarious balance right before your eyes.

The light of the computer screen illuminates this small room, casting a blue glow over his secondhand furniture: the overstuffed "pleather" chair that is held together with duct tape, the large lamps that feature pleated shades and bronze bald eagles, a wooden stereo console (the size of a large bedroom dresser) on which he plays his old-time records and polka collections, and the dining room table that has served him well for over twenty years.

Hanging on the wall behind the table is a large picture of a shallow river winding through autumn trees. The picture is at least as old as I am. It hung in my parents' home, and my dad continued to display it after they divorced. Over the years, I've wondered if the painting was a depiction of an actual place. I think I'd like to find it and fish its rambling waters alone with my dad.

—✠—

Life is simple when someone you love is dying. Days are filled with sitting, waiting, talking, and updating new visitors. At the hospital, we trek to the cafeteria to drink cups of bad coffee and eat slices of stale pizza. We walk outside to breathe the chilly air and remind ourselves that we're alive. Morning becomes afternoon. Afternoon becomes evening. Weary family members come and go. Some leave for the night. Although they want to hang on to every moment, they know they need their rest for what lies ahead.

It's day two of my visit and more of my family has gathered. The day has been long and sad. "Good night, Dad," my cousin Nancy says, kissing Uncle Tom on the cheek. "I'll see you in the morning."

Nancy is Uncle Tom's youngest daughter. One of her many talents is that she can lip-sync Whitney Houston perfectly. Ever since she was a teen, she has "sung" at every family event and has wowed us every single time. Nancy is gorgeous and makes it hard to watch anything else when she's in the room. She has her dad's wide eyes, broad smile, and tall-arched eyebrows. Although she's in her thirties, she's perfectly proportioned and still looks fabulous in a bikini. But she's so vibrant, sweet, and lovable it's impossible to be jealous. You only end up wishing she were your very best friend.

Her older sisters, Margie and Judy, take turns kissing their father, too. What no one says, but everyone knows, is that this—*this*—could be the last time. We don't know how to reconcile that reality.

My sisters stay in the hospital room with Dad and me a little longer, partly because I'm in town and we want to be together. They both have to work tomorrow, so they finally say good night as well. Dad and I are the only ones left. We turn out all the lights, leaving a single muted table lamp lit in the corner. In the hushed stillness, we talk about everything: grandkids, church, and family. We talk about nothing: weather, traffic, and upcoming holidays. We sit in silence. We listen to Uncle Tom breathe.

"It's getting late, Eileen. You need your rest," Dad says.

"I'm fine."

"I know you're fine. But you need your sleep."

"I'm not tired yet. Really," I say, giving him a soft smile.

He stretches out his legs and folds his arms across his chest. His eyes water as he stifles a yawn.

There once was a time when I would not have been able to sit like this with my dad. I would have felt uncomfortable with the silence, and death would have frightened me. But this time is precious to me, and I iron it into my soul for safekeeping. Here we are, together in this moment where beauty and death collide. It reminds me of the line in Thornton Wilder's play *Our Town*, when

Emily Gibbs revisits her twelfth birthday, and says, "But, just for a moment now we're all together . . . just for a moment we're happy. Let's look at one another."

Uncle Tom moans and slightly moves his head. "You need something, Tom?" Dad leans forward with his hands on his knees in case his brother answers. Uncle Tom falls silent again. He hasn't spoken in two days.

"He does that," Dad says. "I just hope he's not in any pain." Dad refolds his hands across his chest and sighs.

I look at my dad and see him. Really see him. He looks young and boyish—much younger than his actual age. He's wearing a white, baggy sweatshirt, his favorite "dungarees," and the expensive sneakers I convinced him to buy to help his arthritic knees. Gray is sprinkled throughout his hair, but he still *has* hair—lots of it—and that's saying something. Truth is, my dad, Clark Gable (yes, that's his name) is handsome. Clark Gable handsome. Everybody says so.

The clock reads midnight . . . then one o'clock . . . then two o'clock in the morning. Time wears on. Uncle Tom continues to breathe. Dad begs me to get some rest, and I finally relent. I bend to kiss him good night and give him a big hug. We both understand the meaning behind my extra-tight squeeze. I walk over to my godfather. "I'll see you in the morning, Uncle Tom." I place my hand on his as I kiss his cheek. I hear only the sound of his breathing. His hand and cheek feel cold.

I drive the twenty minutes from the hospital to my sister's house. There's something about driving in the middle of the night that feels both dangerous and brilliantly clear. Things make sense in the middle of the night, and life seems to work itself out in the shadows. I look around as I drive the streets that I know and love. I've traveled them all my life. This is home.

I pull into Wegmans, grocery store extraordinaire, to buy cereal, milk, juice, and fruit for the morning. I put my items on the conveyor belt, and the cashier begins scanning them. "Sleepover?" he says, weighing the bananas.

I wish. "No. My uncle is in hospice."

"Oh. Sorry to hear that. How old is he?"

I sigh. "He's in his seventies."

"A good run," he concludes as he bags the Tropicana.

"It's still hard," I say. Truth is, it's never a long-enough run. My uncle Tom is someone's dad, grandpa, brother, uncle, friend. How long, really, is long enough? I know a man whose mother died when she was over a hundred years old. Every time I talk with him, he tells me how much he misses her. Only eternity is long enough to spend with the people we love.

—∿—

Daylight arrives. The hospital room gets more crowded. Uncle Tom's breathing has changed, and the time is drawing near. My entire family descends on the hospital to hold vigil in the waiting place together. Aunts, uncles, cousins, grandchildren. We are loud, boisterous, tragic, and (surprisingly) funny.

Uncle Tom would not have wanted all these people staring at him, but he would have loved that the nurses ask repeatedly if he is a celebrity. Our family spills into the hallway and the waiting room, where the younger kids watch *SpongeBob SquarePants* on an overhead television. The older kids curiously peek into the hospital room every so often, wondering about this thing called death. Uncle Tom's room is large and includes a small sitting room. Trays of sandwich meats, breads, cheese, fruits, and vegetables are delivered. By the time I walk in, my aunt Helen, one of Uncle Tom's sisters, is eating a ham sandwich. "Eileeeen!" she says. "How-ah-ya?"

"Good, Aunt Helen," I say, kissing her cheek. "It's good to see you."

I say hello to Andrew Michael, my cousin who has never been able to shake his two first names. "Hi ya, Eileen," he says, kissing my cheek. "You look beau-tee-ful as always." Andrew Michael, Aunt Helen's son, is a perfect mixture of John Ritter and Mr. Rogers. He's always been a sweet, gentle man.

"Aw, thanks, Andrew Michael. How're you doing?"

"Good. Good. You know, considering the circumstances," he says, quietly articulating every syllable like he always does.

"I know," I say, looking away. "I know."

I greet my other family members with a kiss. My aunt Eleanor, whose husband died just weeks ago, is devastated. She's mad at the hospital doctors who told her they believed Uncle Frank would be well enough to go home again. And she's mad at God for taking her "Twinny" after fifty-eight years of marriage. "I'm not sending out Christmas cards this year, Eileen. You won't be getting one from me. And don't you send me one either. I don't want it. I'm not celebrating Christmas anymore."

"Okay, Aunt Eleanor," I say, squeezing her. It's no use arguing at a time like this. She just lost her husband. She's about to lose her brother. Who cares if she doesn't send out Christmas cards?

More chairs have been brought into the main room, filling its perimeter. I take a seat next to my dad and look at the people I love. Susie sits on my left. Dad is on my right. When my mom walks in, everyone is a little surprised. It's been twenty years since my parents divorced, but hey, Uncle Tom was once her brother-in-law. Plus, Mom wants to be where her family is. She doesn't want to be left out. She moves toward my dad. "Hi, Clark," Mom says.

"Hi, Bonnie." Mom extends her left manicured hand to him. He takes it into his right hand for a moment, giving it a gentle squeeze. Mom continues to work her way around the perimeter of the room, greeting the rest of the family, before she takes a seat nearby.

Uncle Tom's breathing slows. A few seconds pass before he draws in another small puff of air. There's no life left in his half-open eyes. Gables are hearty, stubborn Polish people. It's not easy for their bodies to figure out how to stop.

A few seconds pass before he takes another breath. My dad puts his hand on my knee, as though he's trying to steady himself. A few more seconds pass. No breath. Dad squeezes my leg. *This is it.* But then Uncle Tom gasps again.

My dad swears under his breath. He wants his brother's pain to be over, and he's ready to let go. *Please, God: Just take him.*

In spite of these moments, there's still a lot of small talk between family members. It sounds like the murmur of the congregation before a church service begins. Family members are still asking questions and sharing health-related concerns. There's a commotion in the side room near the food trays. Aunt Helen and Andrew Michael are having a spat about his marathon running. "All you care about is that running. You're gonna hurt yourself," Aunt Helen says accusingly.

"Don't start on me, Ma. I'm tellin' ya, don't start on me," Andrew Michael says angrily. He's always such a hi-ya, how-ah-ya, good-to-see-ya kinda guy. It's almost comical that he chooses this moment to get mad.

I look at him and raise my eyebrows. He shifts his attention to me. "So tell me, Eileen. How's Michigan?" I shake my head and discreetly point to Uncle Tom. *Not now. It's time.* "Hey, Ma. You'd better come over here," Andrew Michael says to Aunt Helen.

He helps his mother stand. She hobbles nearer to her brother's bedside. "Ohhh," she says. "Tommy."

My dad's hand is still gripping my knee. I place my hand on top of his, noticing the resemblance between his and Uncle Tom's. It must be sheer agony to watch your brother die.

In this waiting place, I'm reminded of Dad's mortality. I know there will come a day when I'll be the one standing at the side of *his* bed. (Unless, of course, I die first, which would be more than my father could bear.) I can't stand the thought of losing him, but I'd be in denial if I didn't consider it. My dad's so alive now, and we're so close. There's so much to love about him. He's simple . . . the kind of man who takes joy in the fact that he can fix a lawn mower. He's joyful . . . the kind of man who enjoys a cup of coffee, the newspaper, and the evening news. He's easily awed . . . the kind of man who still stops whatever he's doing to watch and appreciate an airplane flying overhead. I feel the strength in his hand as he tenses and releases. I listen to him hold his breath intermittently. Together, we wait.

Uncle Tom takes a breath. Several seconds pass. Dad still grips my knee. Uncle Tom takes another breath. We all groan. Margie, Judy, and Nancy gather around their father. They lean into him and hug him and repeat how much they love him. We think he stops breathing. He breathes again.

Suddenly Nancy turns to our aunt. "Aunt Eleanor, can you hand me Dad's Dopp kit, please?"

"Sure, honey." Aunt Eleanor quickly hands her Uncle Tom's black leather toiletries bag.

"I know what you're waiting for," Nancy says to Uncle Tom.

She pulls the comb from the kit and runs it through her dad's hair. The Gable men all wear their hair the same way, in an ever-appropriate Clark Gable style. Short on the sides and longer on top with a signature swoop. She holds her father's face in her hand and lovingly fixes his hair. She finishes his swoop by rubbing a dab of Vaseline between her palms and smoothing it into his familiar style. "Now they all know your secret, Dad," she says, smiling through tears. She places his head back onto the pillow as he takes his final breath. It *was* what he was waiting for.

The rest of us know we should be looking away. We might be family, but this is a private moment between a father and his daughters. Certainly we should be filing out of the room and closing the door. But we are transfixed and pressed into our seats as tears run down our faces. For most of us, this moment is the single most tender, lovely thing we've ever witnessed. It's intimate and holy. It's not humanly possible to look away from something that beautiful. Uncle Tom traveled all the way to Yugoslavia, hoping to glimpse the Blessed Virgin Mother and experience the holy. He would have been shocked to learn that, for his family, the holiest thing of all was to occur in his very presence. It would have been a story he told—with many more details than this—again and again and again. I can just imagine the delighted look on his face when he did.

20

A Thief in the Night

I am waiting for my (half-dressed) knight in shining armor.

It's 4:12 on a Sunday morning in June. Brad, my not-so-sponta-neous husband, jumps out of bed. It's not unusual for him to be up at 4:12 on a Sunday morning since the soon-to-be-delivered sermon frequently haunts his dreams. Still, he doesn't usually *leap* from our bed as he does today. Most of the time, he lumbers from the covers with the enthusiasm of Eeyore.

But this is no ordinary morning.

In a flash, he's at our open bedroom window, peeking through our sheer white curtains onto our driveway below. "Eileen! Wake up," he says, whispering. "I think someone just stole the chair from our van."

Since Jordan is a soccer phenom, we keep our fold-up lawn chair, zipped in its carry bag, in our van so we can spectate at a moment's notice. "What?" I say, sleepily squinting at Brad.

"Our chair. I heard a car door slam, and I think a girl just stole it from our van. She's wearing flip-flops."

"Flip-flops?" Now I'm mad. I shuffle over to his side and pull the curtain wider to glimpse the thief. I see nothing through the screen. Since I require superpower contacts in order to see much of anything, I probably wouldn't be able to distinguish a human's form from a canine's right now. I squint harder, trying to catch movement—any movement at all. Still nothing.

"Which way did she go?" I whisper.

"That way," he says, pointing down the street.

I peer into the darkness, seeing only shadows. "Go. Get. Her."

"I gotta find my pants." Since he's only wearing underwear briefs—and holey ones at that—finding pants is a really good idea. He slips on his black running shorts, creaks down our wooden staircase, and grabs his keys. I hear him unfasten the chain safety latch and click open the deadbolt. I cannot believe this. We might live in a fairly safe town, but this is the second time we've been robbed here. This time the thief will not steal our loot without a fight.

I watch my almost-naked husband climb into our minivan. I can't see his facial expression, but I can see his bare, chicken-white chest gleaming in the moonlight. I watch him carefully back out of the driveway and disappear. On the Richter scale of pastoral life, this rates a 7.5.

Man, what is up with this place? Early in our marriage, we lived in cities where our car was broken into regularly, but our house was never touched until we moved to sweet, little, suburbafied Davison. The first time was two years ago during the week before Christmas. It was a Wednesday night, and our family had been invited to a parishioner's home for a hot dog roast and neighborhood caroling. On the Sunday prior, Brad had been given a monetary gift, which we had kept inside the card on our bedroom dresser. After we returned home, Brad went upstairs while I headed to the kitchen to make the kids' school lunches. "Hey, Eileen?" Brad called down.

"Yeah?"

"You'd better come up here."

Uh-oh.

"What's up?" I said, entering the bedroom cautiously. Brad and I are comfortably messy people. We're not complete slobs, but we're not above tossing clothes on the floor or piling books in the corner. Christmas is an especially cluttered time because we hide the kids' gifts under our bed.

As I walked into the room, it looked like Christmas morning, with wrapping paper everywhere. Important documents from our firebox were strewn across the floor. *Whoa! What happened in here?*

Brad stood by our dresser with a protective look on his face. "Babe, did you put the church gift somewhere?"

"No."

"It was right here. I put it right here," he said, patting the dresser with his palm.

"Oh."

"I think we've been robbed."

"Oh." I stared at Brad's face as the reality of what he was saying sank in. *Robbed. We've been robbed. In Davison? How weird.* "Well, what should we do?"

"Get the kids together and take them over to Mom and Dad's," he said. "I need to call the police."

Our kids were shaken. Stephen was mad. Kristina was frightened. Jordan was curious. On the car ride over to their grandparents' house, they asked questions like, "How did they get in?" and, "What if they're still in the house?"

I comforted them the best I could, but truthfully, I wasn't sure how the thieves got in. And although I assured the kids that the criminals were gone, I couldn't guarantee it. In the past, I had felt violated when I had gotten into my car only to find that someone had left a gaping hole where our radio had been. But that was in my pre-kids life. This was altogether different. This was our home. This was the place we kept our underwear, stuffed animals, Mother's Day cards, and photographs. To be robbed of our personal belongings—while we were attending a church function, no less—was personal and deeply disturbing.

In all, the thieves got away with over a thousand dollars' worth of cash, gifts, and sentimental belongings. The kids were most offended that the thief had found and stolen their allowances, which they had accumulated in envelopes. At the time, the kids were getting about two bucks a week, and collectively they had saved close to two hundred dollars. The idea that someone would take that money was worse than taking candy from a child. They were also spooked by the idea that someone had been in their rooms, rummaging through their Pokémon cards and rock collections. They wouldn't go upstairs alone again for an entire year.

The church was shocked to learn we'd been robbed. The following Sunday, the board took a congregational offering that more than replaced the value of what was lost. Handy parishioners helped fix a faulty side door and installed new lights over our garage and patio. It would take a while for us to feel safe in our house again, but we certainly felt supported and loved by our church.

—⁓—

I breathe in the night air as I wait by the window, watching down the street as the minivan's taillights fade into the darkness. Every cell in my body tells me to crawl back into bed and enjoy the few minutes I have alone. But I'm a loyal, stand-by-my-man kinda woman. If Brad is willing to chase down a thief, the least I can do is wait patiently for him. From the second-floor window, I'll be the first to cheer him on when he brings home the prize.

I retrieve my old glasses from the nightstand to help me see the night better. If it weren't such an ungodly time, this would be lovely. The temperature is a perfect seventy degrees. The breeze gently drifts through the window, billowing the sheer curtains around me. Crickets chirp, and the birds are singing their morning songs in celebratory anticipation of a brand-new day. It's magical, really. I should get up at this time every morning. But I'm not an early riser by choice. In my ideal world, a more reasonable waking time is a whole five hours away.

I look at my rumpled bed. *Come back to me*, it says. *Come back.*

No, I say. It's not right for me to rest at a time like this. I cannot hog the bed knowing my husband might be risking life and limb to reclaim a chair that our entire family fights over.

In *Letters to a Young Poet*, Rainer Maria Rilke wrote, "Perhaps all the dragons of our lives are princesses who are only waiting to see us once beautiful and brave." Standing by the window in my mismatched pajama set, I figure Rilke was right; I muse that I look a lot like Rapunzel waiting to be saved by her man. Here I am up in my tower (bedroom), searching the forest (subdivision) for my hero to return on his stallion (our minivan). A gentle breeze blows my long, blonde locks (short, brown hair) away from my face. Just like a fairy tale, evil lurks in the dead of night. It must be conquered. Tonight it will be conquered by my knight in shining armor (feral pastor in his skivvies).

Yep. Our life is a fairy tale—in that it's often too ridiculous to believe.

Standing in the light of the moon, I shift my weight from one foot to another. I yawn as I peer down the street, looking for headlights. I imagine flip-flop girl's reaction when she encounters my tall, bare-chested husband. I wait for her guilty, frightened shriek to pierce the night when she realizes she's been caught red-handed. I listen for the echo of my husband's booming voice demanding, "Hand it over and no one gets hurt!"

Instead, I hear crickets and birds and the hum of the distant freeway. *Where is he? Lord, we have got to get some sleep!*

Finally I see his headlights, and he pulls into the driveway. He climbs out of the Stealth Bomber and locks it. He is empty-handed, so apparently he's leaving the rescued chair inside the now-locked van. Oh, how I love him. This man is willing to sacrifice life and limb for our family. This man is willing to give up a night's sleep for the sake of love.

I climb into bed and listen to him toss his keys on the stand inside the door and then head for the kitchen for a glass of water before ascending the stairs and entering our bedroom once again.

"Did you get her?" I ask.

He takes off his sandals and slips into bed. "Nah. Actually, the chair's in the van."

"What?"

"Yeah. It's right there. But I know she got something. I saw it in her arms. I just don't know what it was."

"Huh."

"Listen, babe. You shouldn't leave the van unlocked," he says.

Oh, really. A lecture? Now? "Yeah? Well, you shouldn't go running through the neighborhood naked in the middle of the night," I say, laughing. "It's a good thing you *didn't* catch her. She woulda been terrified."

"Very funny."

We listen to the birds sing and try to detect the melody as we consider the night's events. It's hard to believe our lives have come to this. Once upon a time, we got married knowing we were beginning a grand adventure together. We knew ours would not be a run-of-the-mill kinda life. Ours would be exciting and spectacular, characterized by doing great things for God. We wouldn't allow ourselves to be strapped by children, mundane responsibilities, material possessions, or mortgages.

We were like the couple in the movie *The Incredibles*. Brad was Mr. Incredible, and I was Elastigirl. We were ready to tackle the world head-on and hand in hand. We knew we could handle anything life threw at us. I looked at Brad much like Elastigirl looked at Mr. Incredible when she said, "We're superheroes. What could happen?"

A *lot* happened. My naïveté caught up with me, and I realized that much of life is lived not in the spectacular but in the ordinary, day-in, day-out spaces. Just like Elastigirl, I gave birth to two boys and a girl, each with their own insecurities to overcome and their "superpowers" to discover. Just like Elastigirl, I've glimpsed my rear end in a full-length mirror and found myself sighing. And just like Elastigirl, I've watched the life drain out of my superhero husband as he fights back the darkness and wrestles with the mundane. Too often ours is a goofy, this-is-so-not-the-life-I-signed-up-for kind of adventure.

Real life is like that.

—⟋⟍—

Brad continues to lie on his back, staring at the ceiling. I can feel him blinking. It's now 4:38. I'll be snoring again in no time, but there's no way he'll be falling back to sleep. I roll onto my side, place my back to him, and wriggle deeper down into my nest.

"You know what? I don't think it was a car door," he says.

My eyes snap open. "What?"

"I don't think I heard a car door."

"Well, what was it?" I'm reluctant to roll over. I've found my spot.

"I think . . . I think it was the newspaper hitting the doorstep," he says thoughtfully.

I give up and roll over to look him in the face. "The newspaper?"

"Yeah. I think what I really heard was the newspaper hitting the doorstep."

"Well, was the newspaper outside?"

"Yep."

"On the doorstep?"

"Yep."

"But I thought you said you saw her carrying something away in her arms."

"I did. Now that I think about it, it was probably her newspaper bag."

I prop myself up on my elbows. "Wait a minute. You mean to tell me you just chased the newspaper girl down the street?"

Brad thinks about it for a second. "I think so."

"In your underwear?"

"I was wearing shorts."

"Uh-huh."

I start laughing until the tears stream down my face. "That poor girl. She must've been terrified. She's probably down the street, hiding in someone's bushes right now."

"Probably."

My weekly newspaper column is published on Sundays. Right now, on page three of the Community section, my musings are printed for the world to read. "I hope she doesn't recognize you as my husband. You're gonna get me fired."

"Humph," he says. He lies there a few minutes more, listening to me giggle intermittently. "Well. I might as well get up and get going." He sits up and hangs his feet over the edge of the bed.

"Aw, come on. I'll stop laughing. Please. Give it a few more hours."

"No sense in it. It's okay. I'll be okay," he says, standing once again. "Here we go." And with that, he's off. He's like that Dunkin' Donuts guy who says, "It's time to make the donuts," except with Brad, it's always, "It's time to preach the sermon."

I roll over and sigh, thinking about the night's events. The bed is now mine to hog, but I'd rather have him in it with me. Once again, I'll have to wait for him to come home so I can wrestle him away from his mistress, The Church, and have him by my side for a few hours. I sigh and then smile at the thought of Brad chasing a schoolgirl in flip-flops down the street. In spite of its absurdity, there's no one else I'd rather be sharing this whacked-out life with, and there's no other knight in shining armor I'd be willing to wait for. Whether he's preaching his guts out from the pulpit wearing khakis, or hunting down the newspaper girl wearing nearly nothing, Brad is my hero.

21

LETTING STELLA GO

I am waiting for a ride.

People of faith always say they want God to work in their lives in powerful ways. They want him to move mountains. Call them to great things. Challenge them to a miraculous stroll on top of water and reach out to catch them when they start to sink.

Week after week the faithful stand in churches and sing songs about sacrifice. They pour their hearts out to God and ask him to mold them like clay. They say they want to give it all for Jesus. But let me tell you, when he actually asks you to give up something, and when you have absolutely no doubt that the voice in your head is God himself, it can really freak you out.

It's midmorning in August. My daughter, Kristina, and I are driving home from her optometrist appointment. It is a beautiful seventy-five-degree day. Since my car's air conditioner quit years ago, the windows are rolled down. Kristina struggles to keep her long, brown hair from blowing in every direction, making her resemble Medusa. We are singing along with the Black Eyed Peas on the radio.

We are about two miles from home when I hear the voice in my head say the life-altering words, *Go find Lisa.*

What? Lisa? Now?

Go find Lisa, it says again.

I know exactly who Lisa is. I met her a few months ago when I was subbing in a colleague's public speaking class at Mott Community College, where I teach. When students see a sub walk through the door, they immediately start to grumble, especially in speech class. It's tough enough to build trust with an assigned teacher over several weeks. It's almost impossible to trust a substitute.

I'm a pretty good teacher, though, and I build rapport with students quickly and easily. During class, Lisa delivered her scheduled speech especially well. When I complimented her after class, she thanked me and stayed an extra hour. She shared a piece of her story: She's a single mom of two boys. She recently freed herself from an abusive relationship. She lives on public assistance. Life is hard, but her heart is good, and she's smart to boot. There's always hope, I told her. Through tears, she warily agreed.

Since then her name has been bouncing on my heart. I know she lives in the apartment complex across from the local big box store. I've never been to the complex, but I know there are many apartments, and each one looks exactly the same. I have no idea which is hers.

Go find Lisa.

Okay, okay. Jeepers!

"Hey, Kristina?" I say. "I know this is weird, but I have to do something."

"Uh-oh," she says. (After all, she's known me all her life.)

"I feel like I'm supposed to find a girl named Lisa and ask her if she needs anything."

"Okay. Where does she live?"

"I'm not sure. I guess we'll just have to pray," I say. As we drive up the road to her apartment complex, we pray that God will send Lisa outside her apartment and that we'll be able to give her whatever she needs.

"What if you find her, and she thinks you're crazy?" Kristina says.

"Oh, I *know* I'm crazy," I say, smiling at my sweet-hearted daughter. "But since I think this is what I'm supposed to do, I guess it will be okay."

"If you find her, I'm staying in the car."

"That's fine," I say, pulling into Riverside Pines. "I don't blame you."

Before us, there are dozens of two-story apartments, all painted shades of gray, each with a front door that faces the parking lot. *Oh, Lord. Please send her outside.* I slowly drive up and down the length of the parking lot, looking for Lisa's familiar reddish hair and short, round frame. Instead, I see a guy leave his apartment and drive off to work and a blonde woman chatting on her cell phone on her front steps.

Okay, Lord. Now what?

I gradually work my way up and down the parking lot again, looking for and praying for Lisa. When she fails to appear, I roll down my window and call out to the blonde who has finished her cell phone conversation.

"Excuse me. Do you know a Lisa who lives here?" I ask.

"That's me," she says, confused.

"Oh, your name's Lisa? How funny. Well, this Lisa has two little boys."

"I have two little boys."

Whoa. "And, um . . . she attends Mott Community College."

"Yep. I attend Mott Community College."

What the . . . ? "You do? How weird. Well . . . this other Lisa was in a class of mine a few weeks ago and . . . well, I just need to find her."

"I don't know any other Lisas who live here," the girl says, glancing down the row of apartments.

"Okay. Sorry to bother you," I say. "Have a great day!"

And with that we're off.

"Huh. That's funny," I say to Kristina a few blocks down the road.

"Yeah. Weird." Kristina says. "Maybe she's the Lisa you're supposed to help." Kristina is a pretty smart eleven-year-old.

"I was just thinking the same thing."

We turn the car around and pull once again into the parking lot. This time, no one is outside. And since all the apartments look exactly the same and have no distinguishing characteristics, I can't recall which set of apartments the new Lisa is in. I'm certainly not about to knock on random doors. The idea that God has told me to find someone and ask if she needs help is bizarre enough as it is.

We go home, and Kristina tells her brothers our story. They all agree that I must go back. "You *have* to go, Mom. God told you to," Stephen says.

I wonder if he realizes how wild—and wonderful—that sounds.

I drop the boys off at the library, and Kristina and I head back to the apartment complex, praying. "Okay, Lord. We're gonna give this another shot," I say. "If this is the Lisa we're supposed to find, please have her outside again."

Even before we pull into the parking lot, we see her standing on the sidewalk, carrying a child with strawberry-colored hair. With a quizzical look on her face, she watches us pull in and park. I climb out of the car and walk toward her.

"Hi! It's me again," I say. I'm nervous. My stomach feels like there are geckos fighting inside of it. *What if she thinks I'm insane? Or a stalker?*

"Hi," she says, shielding the sun from her eyes with her hand.

I trip around my mind, searching for the right words. I might write and talk for a living, but I have no graceful way of telling someone that God told me to find her. I just go for it.

"Well, this might sound a little strange, but . . . as you know, I'm looking for Lisa. All I know is that she has two boys and goes to Mott Community College. I feel like I'm supposed to ask her if she needs anything."

She squints at me, trying to decide if I'm dangerous or just really odd.

"I asked God, if he really wanted me to help Lisa, to please have her standing outside. Since you're the only Lisa who has two boys who goes to Mott who lives here, I think I'm supposed to ask you instead."

She raises her eyebrows and shifts her toddler onto her other hip.

I take a breath. "So, do you need anything? Is there anything you need?"

She looks around nervously.

"I know I sound nuts, but I'm not; I swear. I'm a columnist for the *Flint Journal*. And I'm a teacher. My husband is a pastor of a church in this town. This isn't my idea. I really think God wants me to ask you what you need. Maybe I can help."

"Well," she says hesitantly, "I just lost my car . . . so I don't have a way to get around. So . . . if you know someone who's selling a car, I might be interested in buying it."

I light up. *This I can do. Really. Oh, it's so perfect. Outrageous but perfect.*

"I don't know anyone who wants to *sell* you a car, but I might know someone who wants to *give* you one. You see that car right there?" I say, pointing to my Honda where Kristina patiently waits for her mother. "You can have it if you want it."

"Wha—?"

"But it's a stick shift. Can you drive a stick shift?"

"Uh, my car that got repo-ed was a stick shift."

"Excellent. I know she doesn't look like much, but she's a really great car. We call her Stella. We just put a new muffler on her yesterday. She has two hundred thousand miles on her, but she's the best."

—⚬—

It's important to know that Stella is a very distinctive automobile. First of all, I live in General Motors country. The entire region is committed to driving American even though Hondas are often made in Ohio, and GM parts are often made overseas. I regularly have older men stop me in parking lots just to say, "There once was a time you wouldn't be caught dead driving a car like that in these parts."

That's not to say that Stella is impressive. But what she lacks in style, she gains in originality. She's a white station wagon with rust accents. Her navy interior shows every speck of dirt and dog hair. Before we had the muffler replaced, it blew out regularly and made loud farting noises wherever we went.

Even so, I love her. I love her low ride, her easy steering, and the way she smells like McDonald's french fries and coffee. I love her roomy trunk, her squeaky windows, and the fact that I have to whack the back door handle to keep the door from swinging open. Stella is, and always will be, my all-time favorite car.

—⚬—

Lisa is stunned by my offer. "I really don't know what to say."

"I know. It's crazy, isn't it? I mean, I know I'm a complete stranger. But . . ." I proceed carefully here. I'm trying to follow God, not be perceived as a religious whack job. "I think God wanted me to find you today just to tell you he loves you. So if it's okay with you, I'm going to go now and talk to my husband. I'll be back in a few hours. Okay?"

"Um. Okay," she says, wiping tears from her eyes. "I've been praying for a car. I had to choose between paying rent or my car payment. I chose the rent."

"It's okay," I say, giving her a hug. "Now you'll have a car. I'll be back."

Kristina and I pull into the church parking lot and skip into the building. I'm a little anxious about telling Brad that I've given Stella away, but I know Brad. If I truly believe God told me to do it, he'll adjust and support the idea. It's how we try to live our lives. This is church at its best.

Kristina and I blow into Brad's office like a tornado. We are so excited—about doing something so fun, about being used by God in such a practical way, about the fact that God still speaks and compels people to do something outrageous for him—that we stumble over one another as we tell him the story. Brad will later say we looked "like two cats that had been rolling around in catnip for an hour."

"Can we do it, Dad? Can we give away Stella?" Kristina asks.

What's a dad—especially one who is trying to raise kids who seek and listen to God—supposed to say? *No?*

"Of course," Brad says. Then he turns to me and looks at me with puppy dog eyes. "It's Stella," he says wistfully. He knows how much I love my car.

"I know. It's okay. It's just a car, right? It's a good thing to do."

At the gas station, we fill Stella full of gas and clean her inside and out. We feed quarters into the industrial vacuum machine and suck out dirt, dog hair, stray french fries, and M&Ms. We pay five dollars and drive through the car wash. In all the years I've had her,

I've never taken Stella through the car wash. Once a year, I hand wash and wax her, being careful not to rub too hard on her rusty spots. Today she shines inside and out. Even her rust gleams.

Back home, I put together a folder detailing Stella's maintenance history. The newest receipt is dated just yesterday for the brand-new muffler. *Stella, there'll be no farting noises for Lisa.* We fill the folder with gas cards and money to help her pay for Stella's registration, tax, and title fees. I scurry around hooting and singing like a woman gone mad. "Mom, are you okay?" Kristina asks.

"Oh, yeah," I say, giggling. "I'm just so happy."

"You're happy you're giving away Stella? But you love Stella," Kristina says, incredulous.

"I know. But the whole thing's so cool, and we get to be a part of it."

"Well, you're acting a little crazy right now."

How do I explain to my daughter how wonderful it feels to step out of the mundane? That I get tired of waiting for a sign, a message, an answer from God, all the while wondering if I'm doing what I'm supposed to do and living like I'm supposed to live?

How do I explain that, even though there's a cost, this is one of the best days of my life? That even though this decision will force me to wait for rides and be repeatedly inconvenienced, it's one of the best things I've ever done?

We pull into the parking lot again, and Lisa, standing outside, puts down her cell phone. "I've been calling everyone I know, telling them how God has answered my prayers," she says, embracing me. "No one can believe it."

"It's a good day. For all of us," I say. I hand her the folder and explain Stella's maintenance history. I show her Stella's quirks—the back door handle and the trunk handle that needs to be jiggled to unlock. As I sign over the title on Stella's hood, a friend pulls into the parking lot to give Kristina and me a ride home. We drive away, waving. Lisa waves back with the car keys in her hand. I check my throat for the lump that tells me I've done something I'll deeply regret, but it's not there. I feel nothing but joy.

—⁓—

Surprisingly, our family adjusts easily to having only one car. We ride bikes. We bum rides. We walk. Even though Stephen must walk the mile home from the high school many days (uphill both ways), he says, "I like having one car, Mom. It forces us to spend more time as a family."

Whoa!

We're definitely not as independent as we used to be, especially during Michigan winters when the snow, ice, and freezing rain make walking and biking difficult. Having to mooch rides stings our pride, but our dependence on others continually reminds us that we are not alone.

Every time I impatiently wait for Brad to return home before I can get where I need to go, I recall that clear command, *Go find Lisa.* Every time I am inconvenienced or temporarily stranded, I think of Lisa's astonished face. These things help me wait through the holy inconvenience. They also remind me that—in that ordinary moment on an ordinary day—God chose me.

22

BRICK WALLS

I am waiting for a breakthrough.

As we pursue our dreams, we live in the middle of the waiting place, a space filled with what-ifs: What if I'm just wasting my time? What if I never get a chance? What if I'm not good enough? For several years, I wandered through this waiting place, faithfully writing columns, sending queries to magazines, and tweaking book proposals. During those years, the economy slipped into the toilet, the newspaper business imploded, and the publishing industry was forced to shrink-wrap itself. Many people told me, "You picked one heck of a time to become a writer!"

"Tell me about it," I said, and kept writing. Somehow my

column survived, and I clung to it like a life raft. I had a few articles printed in other publications, but most of the time I felt like I was trying to peddle chastity belts in the age of Madonna. I'm not above repeatedly bashing my head against a proverbial wall, but after the hundredth bashing it started to dawn on me: I don't have to do this. I can get a *real* job that pays *real* money. Perhaps it's time to try something else.

—⁊⁊—

I'm sitting in the lobby of the Genesee District Library's headquarters, waiting for my interview. I'm surrounded by patrons who type on computers, select DVDs, and leisurely stroll down rows of books with their heads tilted sideways, reading the titles. Gratefully, I breathe in the musty scent of well-loved volumes and smile as I eavesdrop on a patron who explains a novel's intricate plot to a patient librarian. Being in a library makes me as happy as a dog rolling in stinkweed. I love this place.

My outfit includes my friend Monica's snappy, black and white suit jacket and her too-tight-for-me shiny-black dress shoes. I've finished it off with my wear-'em-anywhere fully lined black pants. My own wardrobe no longer includes interview clothes because being an adjunct professor requires business-casual attire, and being a writer requires nothing more than my jammies. It's odd to consistently borrow other people's clothes for major life events, especially since I'm now in my forties. I should probably consider getting a workable wardrobe of my own.

Today I'm interviewing for the library's community-relations job, a made-for-me role if there ever were one. If it's offered, I'll get to do all the things I love best: write, speak, plan special events, connect with schools and media outlets, schmooze. I believe so strongly in the public library that it would be an extraordinary honor to promote it. After all, I've claimed the local branch as an extension of my home. Since my über-extroverted self finds it difficult to write at home, I write at my local branch several days a week. I call it my office and identify the staff as my coworkers. Librarians are the coolest kind of people because they have all those books walking around in their heads.

Heather, the human resources manager, greets me warmly, and I follow her into the group interview where six administrators wait for me. I have such a natural affinity for librarians, I'm tempted to walk the perimeter of the room, hug each interviewer, and say, "Thank you."

"Welcome, Eileen. Please have a seat," Carolyn, the executive director, says.

"Thank you. It's great to be here," I say, settling into my chair and placing my black vinyl portfolio—the same one I used when I was being rejected by the PhD program—on the table before me.

Introductions are made around the room, and I learn who's responsible for what. "We have a series of interview questions," Carolyn says. "At the end of those questions, you can feel free to ask some of your own."

"Great!" I say with the eagerness of a puppy.

"Here's your first question: What do you believe is the primary purpose of the Genesee District Library?"

The answer leaps into my brain and out of my mouth before I have the chance to thoughtfully edit it. "To teach people to love reading!" I say much too enthusiastically. The interviewers look at me blankly, and I sense I've disappointed them from the start. After all, this is the library of the new millennium. Today's services include everything from tax-preparation workshops to computer training to free movie rental. Still, in my mind, it all comes down to holding a book in hand and being transported to another world. It's one of life's most fabulous gifts.

We dance through the rest of the interview. At its conclusion, Heather walks me into the lobby. "Well, that was refreshing," she says with a laugh.

I'm not sure exactly what she means, but I know I can be a little animated. I'm an energetic woman who pounces easily. Three past employers have given me the same nickname: Tigger. "That was a lot of fun," I say, and I mean it. I love interviews.

"We'll be in touch," she says, still smiling. I can't really tell if she's interested or just amused. I walk out of the building with pinched feet, convinced that Monica's shoes have shrunk a size in the last hour, and drive away in the Stealth Bomber.

As I steer toward home, I sort through the interview, half praying, half talking to myself. *It's a wonderful opportunity, Eileen. You couldn't ask for a better organization. You love the library. Wouldn't it be great to have a steady, somewhat predictable job again? Think about it: a salary and benefits, not to mention the potential for donuts on Friday mornings. And the pay is good, especially if you compare it to your writing and teaching pay, which, if your family had to live on it, would easily qualify you for WIC again or some kind of public assistance.*

I turn onto the highway, telling myself, *With a real job like this, you could pay off the mortgage in a few years. Save for the kids' college. Pay off the orthodontist bills. You could promote authors and great books. You'd be making a difference in the community!*

But then, from a chamber deep in my heart, I hear the word *no.*

The thing that overshadows the opportunity is the fact that my writing life would be in jeopardy. A job in community relations would be a conflict of interest to my weekly newspaper column. I also know I would have little time to write outside of work because it would infringe on the reduced amount of time I'd have with my family. There'd be no, "Not now. I'm writing," if my job takes me away from them. When I'm home, I'll need to be *home.*

I know women who manage to do it all at the same time. They get up at 4:00 a.m. to exercise, work on their dissertations, or write their novels before heading to their full-time jobs. When they return home, they start their third shift of the day, shuttling kids, making dinner, helping with homework, folding laundry, and reading bedtime stories.

I always thought I would be one of those women, but the lifestyle no longer suits me. My sanity demands space for conversations, laughter, friendship, and sleep. I realize that if I'm offered the job, my dream of becoming an author will have to be realized another day, perhaps many years from now.

The heaviness that fills the car is palpable. Before I can move forward, I have a decision to make. I'm tired of banging my head against a brick wall, but what if—*what if*—this time I break through? I remember what Randy Pausch said in *The Last Lecture*: "The brick walls are there for a reason. The brick walls are not there to keep us out. The brick walls are there to show how badly we want something."

What if his profound words apply to me? What if the next article gets published? What if the next book proposal gets accepted? What if all I need to do is work a little harder . . . write a little more . . . wait a little longer? Suddenly, I know I don't want to *promote* authors and books. I want to *be* the author who writes books. It's a risk, but I have to press on.

I call Heather the following Monday. "I'm sorry," I say. "I don't know where you're at in your decision-making process, but I need to remove my application from consideration."

"Oh. Why?" Heather says.

"It's just . . . I realized that I'd have to give up writing to do the job well. I've given it a lot of thought, and I'm just not ready to do that."

"I understand."

Her response relieves me. Even though the job may be offered to someone else, I hate to let people down. "Thank you, Heather. I'm sorry if I've wasted your time. I may be nuts, but I need to see where this writing thing is going. I've got to give it my best shot."

Almost a year later, when Karen Neumair, my literary agent, calls to tell me that Thomas Nelson wants to publish my book, it's everything I can do not to scream into the phone. I mentally talk myself down: *Be professional, Eileen. Be professional.*

"Thanks so much, Karen. Oh, my word! Thank you!"

I feel both ecstatic and terrified. I'm like Robert Redford's character in the movie *The Candidate* when he finally gets elected to the US Senate after a long and arduous campaign. With deep sincerity, he pulls his adviser aside and asks, "What do we do now?"

I ask myself the same question after hanging up the phone. *What do I do now?* I conclude that the answer is found in something loud and a little violent. I head to the garage, grab the mower, and proceed to mow the lawn, the entire time repeating, "Thank you. I can't believe it. Thank you. I can't believe it. Thank you."

After spending years peeking through the tiny windows of the waiting place, I feel like someone has suddenly blown open the doors. The sunlight is blinding—and surprisingly intimidating. I need someone to kick me in the pants and help me move forward. I put away the mower, pick up the phone, and call my most realistic encourager. "Hey, Dad. Guess what? A publisher wants my book."

"What?"

"Yeah, really. I just found out."

"Well . . . great," he says. I hear the hesitation in his voice, and I brace myself for what I know he will say next. "But if I told you once, I told you a million times, everybody wants to write a book, Eileen."

My dad, the realist. "I know, Dad. You always say that."

"It's true. I walk into that bookstore, and there are books everywhere! Everybody's looking. Nobody's buying."

"Well. We'll see, right? I mean, I've been working toward this for a really long time."

Dad laughs. "The other day I saw on the television that even Mike Tyson has a book. And I said, 'Mike Tyson? My Eileen doesn't stand a chance!'"

———

I laugh along with him. "Yeah, but the people who read Mike Tyson's book probably won't be reading mine."

"Yeah. Okay, that's probably true." He pauses long enough to muster up his signature encouragement and then repeats the words he's been telling me my entire life, "Just remember, Eileen: a quitter never wins, and a winner never quits. Don't you forget that!"

Although we're separated by three hundred miles and a phone line, I can see his expression in my mind: squinty eyes and pursed lips. He's simultaneously shaking his finger in the air.

"I won't forget, Dad."

"Anyhow," he says, changing the subject, "did you get your tomato plants in yet?"

(That's my grounded dad. He loves me and supports me, but he's more interested in practical matters.) "Not yet. I usually wait until after Memorial Day."

"Yeah, I know. But everything feels early this year, so don't wait. You don't have to plant your whole garden. Just put a few plants in the ground, and see what happens. You might have tomatoes in July."

"I'll do it," I say gratefully. Whether talking about writing books or planting tomatoes, he gives me the courage to believe I can beat the odds and do anything.

—⁂—

When this book about the waiting place was first conceived, I was so stuck I could barely identify what I was waiting for. Since then, I have learned a lot about the waiting place and have been surprised by its many powerful lessons.

In the beginning, I thought writing this book would help me discover and share the ways to flee the waiting place. Instead, I've concluded that to live is to wait. It's *how* we wait that makes all the difference.

I expect to remain in one waiting place or another for the rest of my life. On the surface of my days, I'll wait in airports, grocery stores, carpool circles, restaurants, and doctors' offices. But on a deeper level, I'll wait for my next inspiration to smack me upside the head . . . I'll continue to wait for my husband to work through ministry issues . . . I'll wait at the bedsides of friends and family as their lives' curtains close . . . I'll wait for my children to go to college, discover their passions, grow in their faith, and make peace with their own waiting places . . . I'll wait for God to tell me it's time to go home.

My waiting places will change and challenge me to grow. They'll overlap one another and fight for my attention. Sometimes a waiting place will be so important it will cancel out everything else. And once in a while, I'll be able to break free.

Through it all, I'll peer into the waiting place's dingy corners and hunt for treasures beneath the grime. I'll embrace the pain, beauty, angst, and joy of this gorgeous life and refuse to concentrate solely on the mundane. I'll seek laughter amid the tough stuff and loveliness in the sorrow. I'll search for signs of God's fingerprints, even when it seems he's failed to appear. I'll spend time with the people I adore and creatively show them how much I love them. And I'll resolve to remember that now—even the most difficult now—isn't forever.

BREAKING FREE

The thief slipped in without my knowing
and skulked downstairs where my busy-ness waited,
I could feel him pacing, pacing, pacing
and heard him speak the words I should not believe:
"You are not good enough."
Buried in my cluttered, dust-filled room
and trembling beneath the suffocating covers,
I peeked out and around only once in a while
to listen and repeat in my unconvincing voice,
"You are wrong, you are wrong, you are wrong."
His confident doubt held me hostage
and mocking laughter blocked the naked stair,
I shivered and pulled my soft shell tighter
knowing my sedentary stance confirmed my worst fear:
I am a coward.
At last, I bolted from my waiting place
and chanced believing the risk might render reward,
I sacrificed my terror to the light and begged it to save me
as the thief's final curse filled the space of my shadow:
"You. Will. Fail."
But he was wrong.

—Eileen Button